BECOMING AN INDEPENDENT INFORMATION PROFESSIONAL

How to Freelance, Consult, and Contract for Fun and Profit

Melissa M. Powell, Editor

Foreword by Loida Garcia-Febo

LIBRARIES UNLIMITED™

An Imprint of ABC-CLIO, LLC
Santa Barbara, California • Denver, Colorado

Library of Congress Cataloging-in-Publication Data

Names: Powell, Melissa M., editor.
Title: Becoming an independent information professional : how to freelance, consult, and contract for fun and profit / Melissa M. Powell, editor; foreword by Loida Garcia-Febo.
Description: Santa Barbara : Libraries Unlimited, 2018. | Includes bibliographical references and index. | Description based on print version record and CIP data provided by publisher; resource not viewed.
Identifiers: LCCN 2017028853 (print) | LCCN 2017036879 (ebook) | ISBN 9781440855412 (ebook) | ISBN 9781440855405 (hard copy : alk. paper)
Subjects: LCSH: Library consultants—Vocational guidance. | Information consultants—Vocational guidance.
Classification: LCC Z682.4.C65 (ebook) | LCC Z682.4.C65 B43 2018 (print) | DDC 023/.2—dc23
LC record available at https://lccn.loc.gov/2017028853

ISBN: 978-1-4408-5540-5 (paperback)
978-1-4408-5541-2 (ebook)

22 21 20 19 18   1 2 3 4 5

This book is also available as an eBook.

Libraries Unlimited
An Imprint of ABC-CLIO, LLC

ABC-CLIO, LLC
130 Cremona Drive, P.O. Box 1911
Santa Barbara, California 93116-1911
www.abc-clio.com

This book is printed on acid-free paper (∞)

Manufactured in the United States of America

Contents

Foreword

Loida Garcia-Febo, International Librarian,
Consultant, and Educator

I'll never forget how impressed I was when my mother told me, as a young girl, that the director of a news broadcast was a librarian. I thought that librarian was performing a great service for the island where I grew up. Knowing that there was a librarian, someone from the same profession as my mother, contributing to keep my fellow citizens informed had a great impact on me. I thought, "Wow! I could do something to help my country too." Although the news director was not a consultant, she was performing a nontraditional library job and that opened a world of possibilities for a young girl from the mountains of Puerto Rico.

Whenever I am teaching students and new librarians, I mention all the different types of nontraditional library jobs someone with a Master's of Library Science (MLS) can perform. There are librarians working in NASA, not-for-profit organizations, nongovernmental organizations, national security agencies, TV stations, and e-commerce Web sites. And many information professionals choose to work as consultants, whether it be full time, part time, or just on occasion. This book is for those who are considering any of these options.

There are many reasons why we choose a career path. For many years I worked as a librarian, consulting in my spare time. Then, some years ago, I took up consulting full time. I love to help librarians and people from other organizations figure out how best to reach and develop services for diverse and underserved populations. In the words of Carson Block, who wrote the second chapter of this book, I have committed my career to values-based consulting. My drive is my desire to help communities and people who might otherwise not receive services. At the end of the day, I hope that my work makes a difference. It is important to me to know that at the core of what I do, I feel a deep sense that I truly believe in what I am doing.

If you are considering becoming a consultant or have already launched a career change in that direction, this book will be a terrific resource for you. It spells out everything you need to decide if library consultancy is for you, as well as how to be a successful consultant.

Feeling comfortable and excited about consulting is important, not only for our performance, but also for our own well-being. The worksheets developed by Nancy Bolt and Liz Bishoff in Chapter 1, "Is Consulting Work for You?," will help you decide which path is best for you based on aspects such as types of consultants, aptitudes, and consulting roles. The job of consulting can be fun, but it is also hard work, so consider the challenges that will affect your personal life and how you might be able to manage those.

I believe in maintaining a balance between everything I do. Families, friends, and self-care are central to continue juggling different projects. Sometimes people ask if I sleep or if there is a magic formula to accomplish everything. I can only say that I try to strictly follow deadlines, but I am very careful to reserve time on my agenda for my loved ones. Project management (PM) methodologies are excellent ways to schedule work and personal blocks of time, as Emily Clasper discusses in Chapter 8, "Getting It Done: Project Management Tips for Library Consultants." PM tools help to clearly map out roles, project scope, and set up the overall stage for success.

Another interesting aspect of consultancy relates to how sometimes colleagues, who might be starting to consult, run into friends who might not be aware that the consultant must be paid. Finding clients willing pay for your services could be a challenge. Travel between cities, presentations to groups, time spent speaking on the phone, meeting in offices, and answering e-mails is work, and as such should be paid, and doing special favors for friends is a path fraught with danger. Identifying people who will pay you enough is key for your business, as Pat Wagner explains in Chapter 3, "The Map of Your Marketplace."

After all, consulting is a job, and the consultant is only securing payment for the work performed. Due to the nature of this job, where the worker gets paid per contract, it will be important to make sure that your pipeline is full. There might be a number of concurrent projects happening, while at the same time, you are actively seeking future projects. It is up to you to decide how much work you can handle. But as Melissa Stockton makes clear in Chapter 7, "Pipelines and Charging for Services," it is also important to think about when and how to say "no." Saying "yes" and taking on jobs could be exhilarating, but delivering on time and getting repeat satisfied clients with good references is best.

All of these aspects are interlinked to the type of company culture the consultant follows. Even when you have a one-person business, there are strategies you can follow to ensure that you accomplish goals and deliver projects on time. In Chapter 5, Jamie Hollier and Tynan Szvetecz mention types of leadership models to consider when consulting. Leadership is demonstrated in your work with your own organization's team and when you win a request for proposals (RFP) to work with a library team. Understanding different work cultures positively affects the relationships you develop with libraries, vendors, and partners.

Some consultants are part of a larger company and others go solo, running their businesses from home offices, coffee shops, and co-working spaces. In either case, it is beneficial to develop a strategic business plan that will help to not only identify various types of clients, but also understand the legal and financial aspects of the consultancy business. Denise Shockley offers you guidance in this area in Chapter 4.

Of course, a key aspect of running a successful organization is to be familiar with the laws and paperwork required by government agencies. Filling out and keeping tax records according to the city, state, or country laws, depending on the scope of your organization, can help avoid roadblocks—and disentangle from them if they should occur. It's critical for you to frequently communicate with your attorney and accountant and keep updated records and paperwork. This way, if any situation ever comes up, everything is in order and readily available.

Today's consultants must establish an effective online presence in the form of a website and/or social media. The strategies used to define personal and business brand are inherently related to successful enterprises. Libraries, universities, and schools have online presences, and it is a natural step for consultants working with them to show their work online as well. In Chapter 6, Crystal Schimpf provides comprehensive advice about how to develop these tools, design a logo, and maintain various social media. She has even included Slideshare, an excellent, if underused, tool to record presentations that potential clients can see as proof of your work.

One message you'll find in this book that I'd especially like to reiterate is to consider professional activities and volunteerism. This not only allows you to gain professional insight, but also to make new connections. At the same time, you'll be helping the profession and the populations we all serve. Many consultants are active members of the American Library Association and participate in its divisions, round tables, and committees. Consider that the Code of Ethics developed by the Association of Specialized & Cooperative Library Agencies (ASCLA) is considered by consultants nationwide when working with libraries. Consultants are valuable participants of the American Library Association (ALA). Maureen Sullivan, ALA president 2012–2013, is a successful, organizational consultant, and I have the honor to have been elected ALA president for 2018–2019.

Recently, someone asked me if ALA was an association for consultants, and I had the pleasure of answering positively. I believe all ALA members bring unique expertise and valuable experiences to enrich our association, benefit its members, and ultimately, benefit the communities we serve. ALA's strength resides in its membership. Being a library consultant myself, I can say that this is a mighty group.

Today's librarians are driving change, and library consultants are right there with them jointly driving this change in cities, countries, and the world. All of us, library and information workers, are key players in powering development and are essential for democracy.

Whichever path you choose, I sincerely wish you success and that the words in this book offer help along the way.

Introduction

How to Use This Book to Get Where You Want to Be

Melissa M. Powell, BiblioEase

So you want to be a consultant? Now what?

This book came about because of the question every consultant gets: "How can I do what you do?" The snarky answer is usually something along the lines of "work for over 25 years in every kind of library in pretty much every department and then come talk to me." However, the genuine answer is the question, "What is your passion?" This always leads to a conversation, usually a long one, because there is no short answer when it comes to career choices, and this is definitely a career choice. A big one. At first glance, being a consultant looks like fun. You get paid to tell other people what to do while making your own hours. What could be better? So consultants who are asked this question always want to make sure that anyone considering this career choice goes in with their eyes wide open to the ups and downs of the profession.

When thinking about *how* to write this book, the idea of having a series of conversations with various consultants morphed into specific chapters from experts in the field with successful consulting businesses. Have them tell stories of their successes—and flops—while conveying pertinent information about different aspects of starting and maintaining your own successful business. What better way to "show it like it is" while giving the best advice for getting started?

The result is this journey through the process of becoming an independent information professional designed to help you make the decision: "Do I really want to do this?" To quote a workshop participant in the first chapter of this book, "I now know for sure that I *do not* want to be a consultant."

However, the intention is not to scare you or discourage you, but to give you all of the information you might need to make an informed and intelligent decision. Would you expect any less from a bunch of librarians?

First off, how does this book differ from other books on starting a consulting business? It contains a lot of the same information you will find in other books like it; however, this book is focused on those who want to work primarily with libraries and have a background working in and with libraries. It is written solely by those who already work in the information profession, mainly libraries. The examples and suggestions all come from the knowledge that you are experienced with libraries and the information profession so they are relevant and specific. It is written specifically for you.

The best way to get the most out of this book is to approach it with an open mind. You may already have an idea in mind of what you want to do. You could already have a plan laid out, and all you want is information on the particulars of starting a business: what to charge, how to file taxes, or how to market yourself. You could just skip to those chapters; however, it is recommended that you start from the beginning and work your way through. There are several reasons for this:

- **Ethics:** Do you know that there is a library consultants Code of Ethics?
- **Values-Based Consulting:** How do you build your reputation and keep it?
- **Challenges:** What are the specific and real-world challenges you will face once you start taking clients?
- **Brand:** Who are you as a consultant, and how do you represent that effectively?
- **Pipeline:** How do you find enough work to keep your business in the black while not taking on too much?
- **Unexpected clients:** Are you aware of all of the different types of prospective clients there are out there?

The answers to these and many other questions you may not know you have until it's too late are sprinkled throughout the chapters of this book. Ideas are introduced and built upon by each successive author.

This book is going to challenge you. It starts out digging into the heart of consulting—its challenges, rewards, ethics, and the necessary skills for a successful career. Once you have gone through the rigorous journey of "self-discovery" and learned about your marketplace, there are the chapters that get to the business nitty-gritty: marketing, branding, finances, legal issues, getting work, and actually getting work done. Even these will challenge you to think in ways you may not have considered before.

Before you even start thinking about setting up your business, you need to do several things. One very important step is to figure out if you have what it takes to be an independent consultant. It isn't like working for someone else, or even being a director. You are on your own now. Do you have the temperament to work with others in a completely different capacity? Do you have the drive to get up in the morning when you don't have to be anywhere other than your own office? Do you have the skills that other people want, and can you share them appropriately? What if you don't like public speaking: Can you still work as an independent consultant? There are many different types of consulting and freelancing out there.

Another idea behind this book is to inform you about the way consulting works now in the 21st century. Edgar Schein, longtime consultant and expert in organizational culture, noted in his most recent book, *Humble Consulting*, that consulting has changed in the 21st century. Clients are looking for consultants who are committed to being helpful, have an honest curiosity, and have the right caring attitude. Consultancy is moving from big diagnosis and interventions to small adaptive moves. Consultants should concentrate on relationship building with their clients and, through that process, move beyond the formality of professional distance and get to the heart of what is really on the client's mind, the root of the issue worrying them (Schein, 2016). How do you, as a library consultant, do this?

Called *Values-Based Consulting* in this book, the ethics behind consulting and building that level of trust as a library consultant are explored deeply—not just in your relationship with your clients, but your fellow consultants as well. It can be hard to stay genuine when you are out there trying to make a living, worrying about where the next paycheck is coming from. There is always that little niggling voice saying, "Just this once you can slide." How do you balance making a living and keeping up with the ethical standards of the profession? Client loyalty is built on your ethics—how you treat those you are working with and for.

Before you can start getting into the nitty-gritty details of setting up your business, you need to figure out who your customers are and how you find them. How do you decide what you are going to do and for whom? Sure, you may have connections and some people anxious for your expertise, but how long will that sustain you? Are you aware that others are out there, maybe not even libraries, that are hungry for what you know as well?

The next step is the part we all avoid: the actual legal and financial aspects of owning a business. Delving into all of the business entities, tax rules, financials, and reports can be daunting; however, they are necessary before you start taking on clients. There are simple and easy-to-follow directions on choosing your business entity, the tax rules for that entity, and the paperwork you need to file, as well as information on bookkeeping and other financial concerns.

Another step in setting up your business is your determining your brand. A big part of that process is understanding your company culture. Having explored your skills, ethics, and passion, at this point you should have a good idea of who you are and what your company represents. Even if you are a sole proprietorship, you will be a certain kind of leader and through that create the culture of your company. You will be a part of teams as you work on contracts. You will hire subcontractors for larger contracts or work in partnership with other consultants. Who are you, and how does it come through in your business? This is what will stay with clients and get new clients. Once you understand your company culture, building your brand is easy.

Of course, building a brand is so much more than getting a logo. It's all about who you are, why you are doing what you do, how you are doing it, and for whom. You spend much of this book exploring who you are, why you are starting a business, and how that business reflects your purpose. Now it's time to take that and apply it all to your brand to determine your marketing, in all of its glorious forms: logos, Web sites, e-mail, social media, networking—pretty much anything you would want to consider in promoting and maintaining your business.

In addition to marketing, how do you get the work? You have already explored your potential customer base and ways to get work by networking; however, there are other ways clients seek out consultants. What are RFPs? How do you get paid? What do you look for in a contract? What in the world is a pipeline, and why should you care? Even how to say no to a client or contract. Yes. You will want to say no. Throughout this book you will get examples of how, why, and when to turn down a contract or even fire a client. There are situations that can damage your reputation, and you need to understand how to recognize them and clean up the mess.

One tool that every independent information professional needs in their toolbox, no matter the type of consulting, freelancing, or contracting you decide to do, is project management. You need to understand how to organize your projects to keep your pipeline full, your projects on task, and your clients informed to have the successful business that you crave.

Before you move on to the first chapter of this book, start with one question and keep coming back to it as you read:

What is your passion?

What is it about the information profession that has made you decide you want to help others? That is the one thing that will keep you going through setting up your business, getting clients, working on projects, and everything else that comes with being a business owner. You need to love what you do on a base level because it can be tough. You are the boss as well as the staff. You will have bad days/weeks/months, and you need to keep tapping into that passion to keep moving ahead. Your passion for what you do will excite others, including your clients, and they will want you to be part of their journey in whatever capacity you choose for your business.

What has inspired you to step out and become an independent consultant, trainer, or freelancer? Are you escaping from a toxic work environment, do you feel you have more to share than you can do in your current job, or are people calling you and asking you for help or advice on their projects? Any of these are legitimate reasons to set out on your own. However, there is much more to think about when starting your own business. As you will read in Chapter 2, this can be more like a calling than simply a career.

Each of these consultants has spent years doing what they are doing, and they are excited to share what they know with prospective consultants. As you will see as you begin working in your new career, consultants like to work together, support each other, and learn from each other.

Look at this book as a series of conversations about different aspects of being an independent information professional from consultants with a commitment to being helpful, possessing honest curiosity, and the right caring attitude. A great way to start you off on your new journey to become an independent information professional!

RESOURCES

Schein, Edgar H. *Humble Consulting.* Berrett-Koehler Publishing, Inc., 2016.

Is Consulting Work for You?

Nancy Bolt, Nancy Bolt & Associates,
and Liz Bishoff, The Bishoff Group

Deciding if consulting work is for you is the first major decision you need to make. At a recent workshop on consulting, a participant approached the presenters at lunch and said: "Thank you so much for this workshop. It was a real revelation to me. I now know for sure that I *do not* want to be a consultant." That's a valid decision. Consulting is not for everyone. This chapter will explore why libraries (or a business or nonprofit) might hire a consultant, four different broad types of consulting, and aptitudes that make a successful consultant. You can choose a type of consulting in which to specialize; you don't need to be an expert in all types. You may not need all of the aptitudes, depending on the type of consulting you use. However, you should feel comfortable and excited about the type of consulting you choose and confident in your ability—or at least be willing to learn.

WHY DO LIBRARIES HIRE CONSULTANTS?

There are some obvious reasons why libraries hire consultants:

- To acquire expertise that current library staff does not have and the library does not want to hire. Generally this type of consultant is hired for short-term projects such as strategic planning or designing and building a new building.
- To evaluate an aspect of library service and make recommendations for improvement.
- To get opinions of an objective expertise to address a problem or issue.
- To determine needs of the community or users in designing new library services.

- To get objective facilitation of a group making a decision.
- To save money, for example, hiring a consultant as a grant project manager rather than hiring permanent staff.
- To undertake extensive research requiring time and expertise not readily available.

There are sometimes less obvious reasons hidden in the obvious reasons such as:

- Strategic planning to help a library develop a way to find more money for the budget
- Facilitation to bring about change in staff performance or attitude
- Board training to overcome conflict between the library director and a specific board member
- Technical services workflow assessment ,which results in library reorganization

As you are recruited for a consulting job or respond to a request for proposals (RFP), know that not all the reasons libraries hire consultants are obvious or stated clearly and need to be further explored if you obtain a contract (see Table 1.1). See Chapter 7 for more on this topic.

FOUR BASIC TYPES OF CONSULTING

There are four basic types of consulting. You may decide to focus on one specific area. However, you will find that in reality they often overlap, and any consulting contract might include aspects of more than one type.

Presenting and Teaching

Today much instruction is done through online courses and webinars. Consultants are hired to prepare these webinars for organizations, including universities and library associations. Some independent consultants, particularly those who have built a reputation for expertise in one or more specific topics, can offer onsite services as well as webinars.

This type of consulting can include being an adjunct faculty at a college or university. Many full-time librarians get a taste of consulting by serving as adjunct faculty. Retired librarians also are often asked to be adjunct faculty.

Because of the talent working full-time in libraries, it is more difficult to be hired to teach or present at library conferences. State libraries, regional library cooperatives, and individual libraries are more likely to have an expert to present workshops. Some exceptionally good speakers receive higher honorariums to deliver library conference keynote addresses. Word-of-mouth promotes

TABLE 1.1. Hidden Motivations in Hiring Consultants

Stated Reason to Hire Consultant	Possible Hidden Motivation
We need expertise the library doesn't have and doesn't want to pay for by hiring staff.	*Staff is reluctant to change; can you make them?*
We have the staff with expertise, but they are busy doing other things.	*I don't like what my staff wants to do. I want the outside expert (you) to tell my staff how to do it right.*
We need help with a short-term project.	*I want this done fast without having to convince staff or upper management that it should be done.*
We want honest opinions from the outside without inside "baggage."	*Staff is fighting. Things are really bad, and somebody needs to say so. Some staff may need to be fired. I want to be able to blame someone else for recommendations that are for major change.*
It's easier to hire a consultant than salaried staff. Also less expensive.	*I'm trying to hide this project from my governing body or union leadership. I don't want them to know what I'm doing.*
It's harder to reject a consultant's recommendations for change.	*There is a preferred solution already. I want you to recommend what I've already decided I will do.*
Help us solve a specific problem.	*My budget is being cut. I can't get a vote passed. I need a million dollars to keep branches open. Help us find the money.*
Facilitate a strategic plan for all or part of the library operation.	*Staff is fighting. Make them stop.*
We want a change agent.	*Staff is reluctant to move into the 21st century. I can't make them change, so you try.*

them from one state to another until they have exhausted the market. The more general the topic and entertaining the presentation, the more likely that presentations will be requested from a broader range of libraries.

Facilitating or Managing a Process

Most consultants have or seek to develop facilitating skills. These are skills that can be used in many different kinds of consulting. Some consultants focus on facilitation by helping groups in libraries make decisions, engage in strategic planning, conduct focus groups or interviews, and/or coach managers or teams. Most of the proposals advertised on libraryconsultants.org are to facilitate a process, either for strategic planning or to help the library select an automation system or assist in building design. Recruitment of a new director is also part of this type of consulting. Some people seem to have natural facilitation skills; however, it is useful to take a course or workshop on facilitation skills from one of the many providers.

Conducting Research or Evaluation

In this type of consulting, consultants are engaged to do research on a topic or evaluate a project, process, or service. Strategic planning often involves research and comparison with libraries or with the library's own past performance. A current priority for many grants is outcome assessment, a specialty in evaluation that looks at the actual impact of a project or service on users, preferably long term. It is part of an effort to measure the impact of libraries on the communities they serve. For example, what is the impact of library programs on workforce or economic development (improved collections on job seeking, workshops on resumes or preparing for a job interview, helping entrepreneurs start new businesses)? This type of assessment goes beyond how many people show up at a program, how many found jobs, or how many actually started a business.

Another aspect of research is the environmental scan. This type of research looks at the multiple aspects of the environment within which the library operates, including political, economic, educational, social, business, and other elements specific to the library. These require researching data sources, making comparisons over time, seeking projections for the future, and relating a community's needs (including academic communities) to current and future library programs.

Surveys are another type of research and evaluation. Consultants survey library staff and individuals who the library serves and assess the results of the survey. Survey questions often include opinions on current services (what works and what might be improved), what services or facilities people might like in the future, and the impact of the service on the respondent. Surveys can also be an element of a broader consulting project, such as strategic planning, designing a new facility, or evaluating a current service.

Unique Expertise

Consultants need to make decisions about what they intend to consult on. Some skills that can be used in consulting are more general, such as facilitating, and others are more specific. The Library Consultants Directory (www.libraryconsultants.org) lists 46 different library consultant specialties, and it doesn't even include more general topics such as customer service or cultural awareness. The field is wide open for new consultants to choose topics that might be of interest to potential clients.

In an attempt to delineate which of these four types of consulting might apply to different consultant specialties, the authors looked at the various types of consulting listed in libraryconsultants.org and attempted to categorize them by one of the four types. They found they could not. All the specific consulting specialties could conceivably include teaching, facilitating a discussion, researching in the context of the client, and, of course, using expertise.

WHAT KIND OF CONSULTANT ARE YOU?

You may be asking yourself: "How do I figure out what I want to do, and can I really do it?" Following are three worksheets designed to take you through the decision process and help you figure out if consulting work is for you and, if it is, what you want to do.

Worksheet A: Deciding Your Consulting Role

This worksheet (see Table 1.2) is designed to help you begin looking at what kind of consulting you might want to do. It lists various activities based on the four basic types of consulting: presenting/teaching, facilitating, research/project evaluation, and unique experience. This should help you think about which of your skills fits these categories and which you would prefer doing.

You may also look at the four basic types of consulting and the list of specific types listed on libraryconsultants.org (see Appendix A). This can help you think about other possibilities you might consider in choosing a type of consulting that suits your interests.

Worksheet A has three columns, two for you to complete. The first column lists examples of the type of consulting you might do. (There is a blank row at the bottom for you to fill in with any you might think of.) In the middle column, indicate if you think you can now do this or if it's something you can learn how to do. In the column on the right, indicate if you would really enjoy doing this type of consulting.

Worksheet B: Aptitudes Important for Consulting

Worksheet B (see Table 1.3) lists a number of aptitudes that are necessary for consulting. Although you don't need all of the aptitudes to be a successful consultant, it helps to have most of them. They can be organized into six broad categories:

TABLE 1.2. WORKSHEET A: Deciding Your Consulting Role

	I can do this now or learn how	I would really like to do this
Presenting/Teaching		
Making speeches at conferences		
Conducting workshops in person		
Designing and teaching courses online		
Presenting reports of studies and projects		
Other presenting or teaching services		
Facilitating		
Facilitating group decision making (planning)		
Conducting focus groups and interviews		
Coaching others to make decisions		
Other facilitating services		
Research/Project Evaluation		
Survey design, implementation, and analysis		
Conducting research on topics		
Program evaluation or study		
Environmental scans		
Data analysis		
Other research services		
Unique Expertise		
Technology, facilities, digitization, special populations		
Project management		
Interim leadership/contract management		
Contract services: reference, cataloging, building planning, informatics, marketing		
Other expertise I have or will learn		

1. Flexibility, including aptitudes such as a high tolerance for ambiguity, able to work in an unstructured environment, creative problem solving, enjoying learning new things (quickly!), and being able to see the big picture.

2. Facilitation skills, such as having an open mind, being a good listener, enjoying working with people, able to explain complex ideas, and able to summarize discussions.

3. Confidence in yourself, including being able to take rejection or criticism, good self-esteem, and able to market yourself.

TABLE 1.3. WORKSHEET B: An Aptitude for Consulting

Attribute	I believe I have this quality	Other people say I have this quality	Other thoughts
Stamina			
High tolerance for ambiguity			
Able to work in an unstructured environment			
Open mind			
Able to take rejection/criticism			
Able to multitask			
Able to meet deadlines/not procrastinate			
Good listener			
Like to work with people			
Creative problem solving			
Honest self-confidence/self-esteem			
Flexible			
See the big picture			
Able to build trust in relationships			
Ethical			
Enjoy learning new things (quickly)			
Able to market yourself			
Humor and perspective			
Able to influence others			
Willing to tell the negative truth			
Able to sum up issues quickly			
Able to think on your feet and make quick adjustments			
Make abstract examples and ideas tangible and concrete			
Able to quickly respond			
Analytical mind			
Facile with numbers			
Enjoy working independently			
Enjoy speaking to groups			
Enjoy teaching and helping others learn new skills			
Like to write			
Optimistic			
Like to travel			
Goal oriented			

4. Good working skills, such as ability to multitask, able to meet deadlines without procrastination, and goal oriented.

5. Ethical and able to tell negative truth to clients.

6. Know your personal preferences such as enjoying to write, to make presentations, or whether you do or don't want to travel.

Worksheet B asks you to first check the aptitudes you feel you have. Check as many as you feel you have or could develop, even if you don't feel comfortable in the aptitude now. For example, if you like the idea of facilitating, there are many options to learn this skill. If the idea of being a facilitator scares you and is something you feel you would never want to do, then pick other aptitudes you can use in consulting. For the second column, think of how you interact with other people. How have they complimented you on your work? Have they recognized your knowledge in an area of library work? Have they mentioned how well you handled a meeting or your knowledge of facilities? The third column allows you to make other comments such as actions to follow up on or information to seek.

In completing Worksheet B, be honest with yourself. If you feel you do not have a certain aptitude, that's a signal to choose a type of consulting that does not require that aptitude. For example, if you don't feel you have facilitation skills or you don't like to travel, you could work with another consultant where you conduct the surveys or do the research, which allows you to work from home.

Worksheet C: Putting It All Together

Worksheet C asks you to "put it all together" (see Table 1.4). It asks you to review your experience and expertise, think about the type of consulting you want to do, and review your aptitudes to do it. Finally, what services would you like to offer? Consider both what you can currently offer and what new skills you might want to learn and offer in the future.

Using These Worksheets

These three worksheets—the type of consulting you think you can and would like to do (A), your aptitudes for consulting (B), and assembling your package (C)—will help you understand yourself and help you determine if consulting is for you and prepare you to move forward. Remember the workshop attendee who went through these exercises and decided consulting was not for her. Although that's a valid response, hopefully at this point, you will be excited about your own talents and expertise and looking forward to learning more details about consulting and how you can put all of these ideas into practice.

TABLE 1.4. WORKSHEET C: Assembling Your Service Package

Review your expertise: Which areas are most prominent? What do you enjoy doing? What do you know well enough that you can teach or help someone else?

Review your aptitudes: What strengths do you have? What gives you satisfaction?

The services you want to offer (or do not want to offer)

CHALLENGES YOU WILL FACE

Consultants love their work, but they do face many challenges. Five of them include: leading a balanced life, dealing with distractions, travel, partnerships, and maintaining your reputation. Also shown are some ways to address these challenges.

A Balanced Life

Many consultants are "Type A+" personalities. They love the work they are doing and don't want to stop. They postpone or interrupt vacations to work for a client. They are teaching an online course and students want their critique, so they carry their laptops and phone with them everywhere and answer client emails late at night. Consulting also affects family members as they work to meet deadlines and travel to meetings. To paraphrase Annie in *Oklahoma*—they can't say no.

Manage This Challenge:

- One advantage of consulting is that you can set your own schedule. Use that advantage to schedule downtime for yourself.
- Tell people, "No, I don't have time for that project" (politely, of course).
- Tell people, "I'm sorry that's not an area where I work" for projects that you don't have the expertise in or areas that you don't like to work in (again politely).
- Try to schedule client work around a vacation for you and your family.
- Try to prepare your family for occasional intensive work periods. Their support for late nights and emergency meetings can be critical.
- Have lunch with an old friend or your spouse.
- Pay for a class or buy tickets to a play so your investment will be an added incentive to stop working and go.
- Do something early in the morning before you get started—take a walk, write a letter, make a casserole for dinner, play your guitar.

Distractions

"I'm sure you can attend our 1 p.m. church committee meeting. After all, you don't have a real job." Every consultant has heard this. Your home as your office is also a great source of distraction.

Good consultants need to be able to focus on their work, ignore distractions around the home office, and tell others that they cannot do nonconsulting work during the day (unless you choose to for a balanced life!).

Manage This Challenge:

- If the exercise class begins at 10 a.m., build it into your schedule so you can get client work done and enjoy the benefits of your flexible life.
- Create an office space where you can separate yourself.
- Give in. Having trouble focusing on the client report you are supposed to be writing?
  - Do the dishes or mow the lawn. Sometimes doing other things helps you step back just enough that you can reframe, recharge, and find a solution.
  - Take a walk, go to a gym, and come back refreshed.
  - Go find somewhere else to work: the library or a coffee shop.

Travel

Consulting can involve a great deal of travel. If your service package includes facilitation, making presentations, workshops, or project or program evaluation, you will need to travel—perhaps extensively. It helps if you are comfortable in airports, airplanes, and hotels and have a high tolerance for delays and changes in plans. You need to be able to work anywhere you can plug in your laptop or tablet and be prepared to have the necessary equipment to connect to wireless and extra power supplies so that you don't let your batteries on all your devices run down.

On the plus side, watch your frequent flyer miles build up! You will know where every ATM machine is at every major airport. You will also learn to be a very efficient packer, so that you always have your overnight kit ready to put in your suitcase. On the negative side, when do you have time to take clothes to the cleaners or have that annual physical or spend time with your family?

Manage This Challenge:

- Use the airport and hotel wireless to get work done.
- Buy a "hot spot" to use when Internet is expensive or painfully slow or not available.
- Use airport services—get a massage, shop for clothes or presents, buy necessities.
- Get exercise—use the hotel workout facilities.
- Order room service and curl up with a good book.
- Bring survival food and eat when you get a chance.
- Put airline, hotel, and rental car toll-free numbers in your cell phone so you can make or change reservations if you're stranded; don't stand in those customer service lines.

- Use one online travel service (Expedia, Orbitz, American Express) so that you become a VIP; they can help you out when flights are cancelled.
- Sign up for the car rental reward programs (Thrifty Blue Chip, Hertz); your car is waiting for you.
- Get airline club cards—pick one to move your status up quickly.
- Never put your work folders, handouts, or project information in your checked luggage. You can always buy more clothes and toiletries, and it makes a good story.

Partnerships

Your personal work style may dictate whether or not you prefer to work with other consultants. Even if you are a "lone wolf," you may be surprised to find that you sometimes enjoy working with others. If you strongly prefer working with others, your client may only have money for one consultant and you may have to work alone or turn down the job. Established consultants may have trouble trusting newer consultants to meet a high standard, whereas newer consultants may find it difficult to prove their worth to established consultants.

Here are different types of partnerships:

Lone Wolf

These consultants don't want partners and don't need them. They work alone unless they encounter a situation where they have more work than they can handle and are forced to subcontract with someone else.

Plus:

Simple decision making; maximum flexibility for the individual; strong identification with the style and expertise of the individual

Minus:

No backup for emergencies; limited ability to grow the business; lower potential for innovation

Occasional Partner

Individual consultants hire partners as subcontractors to work on projects as they need additional help or expertise. The lead consultant may decide to share the income from the contract equally or take a larger or smaller share, depending on the expertise needed and the amount of work to be done. The lead consultant may decide to give the partner equal credit or less. If you are the consulting partner, clarify the budget and credit in advance.

Beginning consultants may gain experience by partnering on one or more projects with more experienced consultants. How do you do that? You need to demonstrate qualities that bring your own expertise, creativity, work ethic, and teamwork abilities to the attention of those with whom you want to work, perhaps by participating actively in the American Library Association (ALA), writing articles, or presenting workshops.

Plus:

Subcontractors add expertise and innovation; capacity to handle emergencies or expansion of business; size and composition of consulting team can change depending on particular needs of project; may lower cost when less experienced consultants are included

Minus:

Must invest time in locating and integrating subcontractor into business; busy subcontractors may make scheduling difficult; possible conflicts in approach

Partnership

Two or more consultants form a partnership and work together on all projects. Some partnerships have been in business for many years. The partners' expertise and work styles are complementary. It's like a well-functioning marriage. Other partnerships last one project and end—too often with recriminations.

Plus:

Partners have different expertise and personality styles; efficient scheduling; regular interaction strengthens coherence of approach; capacity to handle emergencies and business expansion

Minus:

Disagreements may lead to dissolution of partnership or entire business; potential for staleness after a period of time

Whether you are working with another consultant for a single project or contemplating forming an ongoing partnership, make sure you settle key aspects of the partnership before you agree:

- Do you like your potential partner?
- Do you have the same or complementary work styles?
- Do you trust your potential partner to fulfill commitments on time?
- When you have worked with your potential partner in the past, have the results been better than you would have created alone?

- Can you and your potential partner work through disagreements and arrive at the best solution for the client?
- Have you agreed on financial arrangements? Do they seem fair to all?

You will find more on the business aspects of forming a formal partnership in Denise Shockley's Chapter 4.

Maintaining Your Reputation

Because you are working on weighty issues, frequently with substantial power, money, and jobs involved, you will occasionally find yourself in situations where conflicts of interest, confidentiality issues, or financial situations arise. The bottom line is to be honest and ethical in your commitment to the client, in your contract, in the financial arrangement you make, and to the public and the profession. This is covered more in depth in Carson Block's Chapter 3 on value-based consulting.

Manage This Challenge:

- Review the ASCLA Code of Ethics Statement http://www.ala.org/ascla /resources/codeofethics (see Appendix B). It is a useful guide for library consultants regardless of the particular services offered.
- Call a trusted friend or colleague and get advice.
- If you feel your client is asking you to do something unethical, clarify the situation immediately. Sometimes clients may not realize that they are placing you in an unethical situation.
- Seriously consider withdrawing from the contract if the client fails to address your concerns.

Dealing with Negative Recommendations

It happens—sometimes a client does not like the product you provided or the facilitation you did or the workshop you presented. You discover that this client has given you a negative recommendation and thus caused you to lose another project.

Manage This Challenge:

- First, get up your nerve and call the client. Confront the situation and ask why you were given a negative recommendation. Ask if there is some way you can correct the situation. Try and heal the wound.
- Second, immediately remove the job from your resume and any other place where it appears over which you have some control (Google probably isn't one of them). Make sure the individual is not listed as a reference anywhere.

- Third, take the individual's opinion to heart and reflect on whether you did less than your best and whether you should change any aspect of your consulting to provide higher-quality services to other clients.

Delivering on Contracts

If you take on too much work, you may find that you miss deadlines with one client in order to meet deadlines of another. Clients may feel it's okay for *them* to miss a deadline, but rarely allow you to. If your work depends on their providing information or feedback, your carefully organized schedule for all clients may be upended by a delay from one. Potential clients in the library field do talk to each other, and a reputation for not performing can quickly become public knowledge. For more on managing your projects, see Emily Clasper's Chapter 8.

Manage This Challenge:

- Make sure you and the client have the same expectations of performance and that these are outlined in a contract. Discuss at the first meeting with the client.
- Deliver quality work on time or early.
- If you cannot make a deadline for whatever reason, get in touch with the client as quickly as possible, explain why, and renegotiate another deadline.
- If the delay is due to the client's failure to deliver needed information or feedback, negotiate a deadline that says you will provide what is required within XX days of receiving information from the client.
- Add value to the project by providing something above and beyond that doesn't cost you any or very little money.
- At the end, confirm the client is pleased and ask him or her to serve as a reference.

Summary

You will face these and other challenges as you conduct your consulting business. Remember the aptitudes of flexibility, solving problems, etc. Face the challenges and deal with them and move on to your exciting projects.

2

Values-Based Consulting

Carson Block, Carson Block Consulting, Inc.

What I Believe
I believe libraries are unique: they serve the public good by connecting all people to information that educates, enriches and entertains—and at no direct cost to the patron.

Libraries are also a place where people are free to learn, to gather, and to share.

In the information age, libraries are the only institutions that have the interest, culture and expertise to serve citizens by delivering expert and impartial access to information. Taxpayers across the nation agree: libraries are worth it.

For these reasons, I believe libraries are vital to a healthy society.

(www.carsonblock.com)

WHAT IS "VALUES-BASED CONSULTING?"

Values-Based Consulting is based on a simple premise: what a person believes—including their value system, orientation to the world, personal integrity, and more—matters. Not to be confused with the singular "value-based" consulting (which is the concept of charging clients for the monetary "value" of the services offered and often cited as a sure path to making gazillions of dollars by only working 12 minutes or less per week), Values-Based Consulting is about having a strong sense of right and wrong and pursuing opportunities to change the world for the better as part of the daily work of consulting.

Consultants often have a rare opportunity to be in the right room, with the right people, at the right time. Values-based consultants use that opportunity to say or do the right thing to help the right things to happen. If you've been keeping track, you've probably noticed a lot of *rights*—doing the right thing in any given situation certainly relies on skills and is also steeped deeply in a person's personal values. This makes the consultant's contribution very important to ensure that the opportunity to do right wins—and that wrong directions are avoided. This also means that for clients, it's key that the consultant's values are aligned with yours.

Being able to express values through day-to-day work is at the core of Values-Based Consulting. Although there is little to nothing written about this idea (with the closest concept perhaps being values-based leadership), value-driven actions are common and are at the core of all passionate people in all walks of life and all human endeavors.

> Through everyday activities, many of us pursue opportunities to express our passions, and the most fortunate among us can make it our life's work.

Through everyday activities, many of us pursue opportunities to express our passions, and the most fortunate among us can make it our life's work.

Do you love helping people build their own capacity to overcome roadblocks and achieve their dreams? That's what librarians (and teachers) do every day. If you aim to serve librarians as a consultant, your own personal passion for building the capacity of others is key.

Beliefs are not always the first thing people think of when describing the work of consultants.

To quote one consulting mentor—a well-respected giant in the library field—"no one cares what you believe—they only care about what you can do for them."

Another consulting mentor—also a well-respected giant—stated "what you believe is probably the most important asset that you have as a consultant."

In their own ways, they are both right. Words without actions are indeed just words. But for many, words and actions start with thoughts—and at the core of thoughts are beliefs. The world, especially now in the era of ubiquitous social media, is filled with voices broadcasting beliefs (mostly in increasingly specialized echo chambers), but often without any real action to move them forward into the realm of impact.

Values-Based Consulting is an extension of who a person is and how they express themselves in the world and is always centered around doing the right thing. Are you wondering if this describes you? Here's a simple self-test: ask yourself if you would you take the same action in a similar situation whether you were paid or not? If your answer is "yes," then you may already be a values-based consultant!

"I WANT TO BE A CONSULTANT"

In this book you'll have an opportunity to read about many aspects of consulting, including the business side, the lifestyle, required skills, and even the temperament of those who have the best chance of being successful in the profession. As you will gather, it's quite an unusual lifestyle, and certainly not for everyone. In short, the reality of consulting for a living is often quite different from what many imagine.

Many consultants, despite their focus, share a similar experience. It usually comes in the form of a request—from friends, acquaintances, and strangers—that starts like this: "I'm sick of my job and I'm considering becoming a consultant. Can I ask you a few questions?"

When you are starting out, consulting, and especially library consulting, is not the sort of lifestyle that most people picture. For those dissatisfied with their current jobs, consulting can seem like the perfect path to a glamorous wonderland of a life. After all, don't consultants simply get paid—and big bucks at that—for their opinion? The travel is awesome, right? And you get to set your own hours? That has got to be fantastic! And you drive a sports car between caviar and wine tastings on the road, right? Well . . .

Here are some responses to the most common questions about consulting. As you read through the answers and consider what this might mean for your own lifestyle, you may begin to see why values can be such an important driver in choosing this profession.

Q: Consulting means getting paid for your opinion, right?

A: Indeed, consultants are paid for their opinions, and that is an honor. To be a good consultant, your opinion needs to be spot on, every time, and you need to be skilled at expressing it in writing and verbally and in many different contexts. The more *spot on* you are in your opinions and the more skilled you are in expressing them, the more your services are worth—and the more you might be able to charge for them. But no one is *spot on* all the time. Indeed, this is a conundrum.

Q: I love to travel! Is it fun to travel as a consultant?

A: Many of us love the fun and adventure of travel, but traveling as part of day-to-day work is a far cry from pleasure trips. Keeping travel expenses to a minimum is important, so modest means of transportation and simple accommodations are the norm. Travel takes time, so many consultants spend every available second trying to fit work in along the way—for example, taking multiple mobile devices to get work done, including a phone headset to have a fighting chance to hear (and be heard) on what are most often horrible telephone connections. Much of the travel time is spent in motion (or waiting to be in motion), in the library you are working for (often in meeting rooms and offices), and in the hotel with little opportunity to otherwise enjoy the wonderful communities you are visiting. Not all trips are a grind, but busy consultants rarely have time to see the sights or spend much time enjoying local culture.

Q: As a consultant, do you get to set your own hours?

A: Yes, you do get to set your own hours—but they are less flexible than many imagine.

When considering the consulting life, what many people don't see is the actual work involved. As you will see in the subsequent chapters, there are many levels of consultants in libraries, such as staff consultants for a state library agency or regional library system; however, being a consultant for hire means you are a business owner, and your business is helping clients solve some of the most vexing problems they face. Each job is a big job, despite the monetary value of the contract.

For busy consultants, workdays and workweeks tend to be extra-long, with 10- to 12-hour work days being the norm, but often stretching well beyond, especially on travel days. Sometimes you may work a number of weeks without a single day off, and even when you don't, a workweek will typically cover six days. For some jobs, you won't see a check until three to four months after the services are performed (and in some cases, longer), meaning that expenses such as travel will be spent well in advance of being compensated. A big part of the workday is tied up with logistics—scheduling meetings, planning, writing follow-up communications, and more.

For consultants who work outside of their hometowns or regions, the logistics of travel can be a major part of the workday. Traveling as a consultant generally means long days on the road. Finding time to sleep becomes a constant hunt, with even 20 minutes between boarding a plane and the bell indicating it's okay to open your laptop and get to work being prized relaxation time. Hunting for healthy food becomes a preoccupation.

On some days, up to 70 percent of your time might be spent on the *business* of being a consultant, leaving about 30 percent for performing the work you were hired to do and accounting for what you are able to bill for to earn your living. There really are no typical days, though. When on deadline for documents or a day stacked with meetings, it's 100 percent consulting work. Other days, such as ones spent preparing responses to requests for proposals (RFPs) or preparing for and participating in interviews with teams, zero consulting work gets done—and zero dollars are earned. In both cases there is no guarantee of work coming from the effort.

And then there is the financial side for being a consultant for hire who relies on consulting for their primary means of income. When not busy, you worry that your family will starve. When you are busy, you can feel inundated and live in daily fear of not performing/not delivering on time or with poor quality. Whether busy or not, you are also preoccupied with filling the pipeline with upcoming work.

At this point in the conversation, the person with the questions begins to get a little frustrated. Who can blame them? They expected to hear about how freeing the shackles of a 9 to 5 job led to a carefree life of consulting filled with fun, adventure, freedom, and riches. I remember one person in particular saying, "You're making this sound like it's a terrible choice. Why did you choose to become a consultant?"

What a great question.

Although consulting isn't particularly glamorous, if it helps a person pursue their values, it can add up to a wonderland of a life. For example, by not being tied to one place, you get the opportunity to see so much, including how different libraries approach similar problems and issues; how different regions do things; and the truth about communities, regions, and entire states that can only be learned from time on the ground. That alone, which can only be gleaned from visiting lots of places and seeing lots of things, offers a rich perspective to change your world for the better.

AN EXAMPLE OF VALUES-BASED CONSULTING IN ACTION

One of the most rewarding examples I can share about how my values and passions line up with my work as a consultant was a job that wasn't easy but had impacts that still put a smile on my face every day.

In 2015 I won a contract from the Texas State Library and Archives Commission to provide technology training for libraries in rural Texas. If you've ever been to Texas, or perhaps even seen it on a map, you may have noticed it's a very large state (the second largest in the union, much to the pride of Alaska). The job itself, teaching rural Texas library workers (mostly nontechnologists) how to master their data networks, seemed intriguingly impossible. The schedule promised to be grueling—with training locations spread across the state with long drive times in between communities. The longest of the drives was about five hours, but even the prospect of more modest hauls (two to three hours) after a long training day would make some people turn the other way.

One of my core values is to help others build their own capacity, and I try to extend that value in all of the consulting work I do. Sometimes it's appropriate to just perform a task for your client, but often the best route is to teach folks how to tackle problems. Having deep experience in serving rural communities, I know that most of the people I've worked with in small-town America are hungry for such teaching and immediately harness it to make positive changes. Doing much with little and applying lots of elbow grease is a hallmark of rural America.

Rural libraries are also in great need of technical help. Some small libraries are fortunate to have high-quality technical assistance at hand—whether with a staff member, a partner, or a vendor with great tech chops and who has the library's best interest at heart. Many others, though, have nothing of the sort. In some cases, the library has no technical assistance to rely on at all. In other cases, the library is saddled with technical "help" that is anything but: poorly skilled, careless, or downright antagonistic technical support. In the end, library users and the entire community suffer. This situation is just wrong.

The opportunity to right some of these wrongs and help build the technology capacity of libraries to serve patrons across such a large area was irresistible to me and spoke directly to my values. I didn't care about how hard the job would be or how difficult the traveling conditions might be. I knew in my heart that I had to do this.

I discovered that not only was it possible for nontechnologists to grasp the technological concepts, but many mastered them to the point of being able to improve their electronic services for patrons as a result of the training. The stories of creating the curriculum and traveling (with my Texas State Library and Archives Commission (TSLAC) partners Holly Gordon, Henry Stokes, and Cynthia Fisher), the transformation of class participants from unsure students in the morning to feeling like tech masters at the end of the day, and the specific stories of community impacts are best left to another time and place. I can say that every ounce of energy that I—and others—poured into this project not only met the project objectives, but also gave me a level of personal and ongoing joy. I feel beyond fortunate to do work—this and other jobs like it—that align with my values and skills.

THE WHY OF VALUES-BASED CONSULTING

For a values-based consultant, clearly identifying the problem that you want to help solve (in the greater sense, the big problems facing the world or profession) and having the skills to make an impact are probably the most important aspects of the job. It also makes the more arduous and mundane tasks and activities described earlier well worth the time they require.

A favorite example of keeping the big picture in mind is typified of the story of the three bricklayers. Each one of them was asked what they were doing. The first man answered gruffly, "I'm laying bricks." The second man replied, "I'm putting up a wall." But the third man said enthusiastically and with pride, "I'm building a cathedral."

In the process of the simple tasks that mirror the laying of bricks or the building of a wall from the story, a values-based consultant endeavors to build a cathedral. Applying this concept to my own work, I believe every person in the United States (and the world, for that matter), no matter where they live, should have broadband access to the Internet. For many communities, especially in rural areas, the library may be the only place with free Internet access. When I help rural libraries obtain access to the Internet or fix issues with their data networks (including mundane, detailed tech work), I'm helping to "build a cathedral" that I feel should be built!

How Does This Play Out?

A consultant's values, and their skills at expressing those values, can be a driving factor in their work despite their personal style and approach to consulting.

Although little in life is truly binary, there tend to be two predominant traits among consultants: those who spend more time *talking* and those who spend more time *listening*. Values-Based Consulting can be present in either style.

The Talker

Sometimes known as "the sage on the stage," the talker generally has a wealth of knowledge and views interactions with the client as an opportunity to share what they know, often in a one-way fashion. Talkers often have deep knowledge and experience and feel strongly about the correct way to approach a problem. When someone uses the term "sage on the stage," it tends to be delivered in a slightly derogative tone, with the insinuation that it's an anachronistic approach with egocentric overtones. In unskilled hands that characterization can certainly be true, but there are positive examples of the style as well. Favorite examples tend to be spiritual leaders, typified in the recorded teachings of Jesus and Buddha. Favorite fictional examples are how a sensei or teacher is portrayed in popular media, such as the *Kung Fu* television show from the 1970s.

The Listener

Sometimes known as "the guide on the side," the listener generally assumes the role of a facilitator. Listeners certainly have strong outlooks as well, but take a different approach to client interactions. Listeners spend more time, well, listening to clients and generally prefer a "coaching" approach to interactions. When working with groups, listeners generally endeavor to guide groups to consensus. In the Internet age, when people rightfully have higher expectations of participating in decisions and actions that affect their destiny, the "guide on the side" approach has enjoyed growing popularity, especially in teaching situations. In unskilled hands, however, this approach can be used to avoid making decisions, and worse, ducking necessary action and accountability.

Which one is better: the talker or the listener?

It may be tempting to pick one of the two as better or worse, but if so, there's a danger of oversimplifying. Both can be good or bad, depending on the consultant and the needs. In the end, if the consultant's core values are aligned with serving the needs of the library, either style can be effective. If core values are not aligned, neither style would be a fit.

In truth, any good consultant who aligns their work with their values should have the ability to quickly understand new situations and start forming possible solutions almost immediately as they are learning about the situation. Whether a talker or listener, both should be asking clarifying questions, but each will express their thoughts a little differently. The talker might begin offering possible solutions right away, in the form of instant analysis and trial balloons, whereas the listener tends to spend more time in the information-gathering stage by asking questions and listening deeply to a variety of sources before suggesting possible solutions.

Regardless of personal styles, consultants are often brought in to be a part of the action. Sometimes that's recommending a course of action for the client, and other times (and with the blessing of the client) it is stepping in to take action. Good consultants have mastered skills in both being *talkers* and *listeners*

> A good consultant can help a client explore a continuum between several possible solutions to a problem.

and more importantly possess the discernment to know which style to use in any given situation.

A good consultant can help a client explore a continuum between several possible solutions to a problem.

Thinking for a moment of this continuum as a line with two poles, and neither pole is necessarily *right* or *wrong*, there is a lot of gray area to explore with a skilled and trusted partner to weigh the pros and cons of a solution.

For example: let's say you are working as a technology consultant. An organization wants help with increasing the effectiveness of its information technology (IT) operations. The conversation may start with the library director saying something like, "Our IT department is a mess. Nothing is getting done. We have boxes of unopened computers that have just been sitting there for a year, and our systems are constantly going down. I'm not getting e-mail I'm supposed to be getting. There's always some problem, and our board packet is not getting done on time. Help!"

Indeed, help is needed, and sometimes the person calling has an idea of what they want done. If they are angry over the situation or in conflict with one of the players, they often want a recommendation or the consultant to administer discipline to shake things up. Those not experiencing anger or conflict with staff often want gaps identified and perhaps coaching for the staff to get a better performance. Others have found technical flaws in the system and want help fixing them.

In situations like this, it is the consultant's job to confirm any issues, and not just weaknesses, but strengths as well, discover any new concerns, and understand them from multiple perspectives. Most library IT departments have several important groups of stakeholders, minimally including library administration or leadership, library staff, and sometimes patrons (when IT serves patrons directly in some manner). If the IT department is made up of more than one person, IT staff is also an important stakeholder group. In larger library systems, often specialized departments and staff groups need to be part of the discovery process to gain a 360-degree view of the situation.

Next, the job is to determine the root cause of the issues and make recommendations and/or take actions to fix them. At this point you might guess that the root causes of some of the problems described by our library director are technical, but many others might be people issues. If you guessed that most library technical issues are a mix of people and tech issues, you are correct.

This example underscores the importance of values alignment between the library and the consultant. Taking even a relatively simple journey like this one, trying to solve difficulties in the effectiveness of the library's IT efforts typically touches a lot of people and often ventures into sensitive areas. On this journey, it works best to have a consulting partner who has the ability and capacity to understand the nuances and dynamics of the library while bringing both technical expertise and a strong sense of right and wrong to the table. Some may view the problems and solutions in an overly simple manner (i.e., "Someone isn't doing their job and needs to be let go"), whereas a values-based consultant will focus on a more complex approach of discovering and considering all of the factors that lead to the root cause of the problem (some of which may not be simple fixes) to create outcomes that serve the library best.

YOU ARE THE FUTURE OF VALUES-BASED CONSULTING

Perhaps you have searched the Internet for "values based consulting" and, finding next to nothing, thought, "Did this guy just make this concept up?" Well, no. Many admirable consultants working today and many who have come before have always expressed their values through their work. However, as of the writing of this chapter, there doesn't seem to be much *written* on the subject—yet!

Library work, like other professions based around people helping other people, is special. The bottom line of success in a library is not financial profit through the return on investment of dollars, but in the *return on investment in people* by fostering thriving individuals and entire communities by providing no-barriers access to credible information, ideas, literacy, enrichment, spaces, tools, and people. Library consulting should be even more special. Because libraries hold such an esteemed and trusted role in our society, any consultant helping libraries has even more personal responsibility and accountability to do the right thing. In consulting for businesses and industries, a consultant most often has the opportunity to help their clients make more money. In libraries, a consultant has the opportunity to help a library transform lives and build better communities everywhere.

This does sound more like a calling than a profession, doesn't it? That's the point!

If you are a consultant, or if you aspire to be one, you probably already have a good sense of your skills and your aspirations. If you haven't yet, next dig deep into your own values. Ask yourself what you believe, why you believe it, and how those beliefs might influence and guide your work. Share those beliefs through blog posts, social media, and especially in person when you're consulting. Be brave and allow your values to shine through in everything you do and every interaction you have. Write the next chapter and make it known that library consultants are different because their aim is making a difference based on their values!

FURTHER READING

ASCLA Library Consultants Code of Ethics. *Appendix B*. http://www.ala.org/ascla /resources/codeofethics

3

The Map of Your Marketplace

Pat Wagner, Pattern Research, Inc.

PART ONE: THE INDEPENDENT POINT OF VIEW: IT'S DIFFERENT FROM BEING EMPLOYED

Imagine you are planning to move to a new country—that of the independent library consultant (or trainer or coach)—perhaps after having been employed at a "real" library job for years.

Know that you will have a sense of urgency regarding your income that you might not have had when you counted on a steady library job. Every day, whether or not you are earning money while working on a current contract, you'll be thinking about future assignments. Who will hire you next? Will they like your work well enough to recommend you to your next customer? What about next week, next month, and next year?

What you need is a map of your new country to help you identify and find clients within the worlds of libraries and related workplaces. You will discover where to apply your skills within public- private-, and nonprofit-sector enterprises as well.

Success is simple: you need to find people who will pay you what you require, which is different from finding people who like you personally or your services. Just because someone is excited by your ideas does not mean they have the authority to hire you or the funds to pay you *enough* to make a contract worth your time and attention.

There are plenty of customers willing to pay you *something* for your services. Paying you *enough* means that you'll be satisfied with the results of the equation that qualifies the customer as profitable: the amount of money you are paid minus your expenses for the specific contract, the fixed overhead for running your business, and the time and effort it took to net that profit.

Unlike looking for one job with steady hours and benefits, as an independent consultant you will have to find and satisfy dozens, if not hundreds, of individual prospective customers over time. You will have to negotiate each contract from scratch, including the content and scope of your services; the customer's expectations and goals; timelines; and dozens of legal, financial, and logistical details, from which airport you fly into to local tax requirements.

Does this same sense of urgency apply after you score a long-term contract? Big contracts can last months and can provide temporary financial and emotional security. But you still have to plan how you're going pay future bills when that long-term assignment ends. If you don't invest time in outreach to new customers even while immersed in the daily details of current projects, you can fall into the exhausting "feast or famine" cycle. This is true even if you are a good money manager and can save for periods of contract drought.

What is most dangerous is when you have a run of good fortune with new clients lining up at your front door and you neglect looking for future connections. Prosperity can disappear very rapidly.

Being an independent business owner means always looking for that next opportunity even while you are working on your current project.

The Ideal Customer versus the Real Customer

Some people are lucky enough to have a very focused skill set that is suited to a well-defined, easy-to-identify, and local cohort of prosperous customers. If this applies to you, you can fall for the fantasy that the need for your well-compensated skill set will be guaranteed. Forever.

Let's say you are an expert regarding the cataloging of Russian language collections during the Cold War for federal agencies with unlimited funds to fight Communism. Or a subject matter expert in the classics of Roman and Greek history, art, and literature. Or knowledgeable in specific software used to power a popular database management system.

The Cold War ends, universities close down their classics departments, and the database's company is bought and their signature software is discarded by the new owners.

Some people liken this dream of the eternal customer—the one you find once and sign forever—to stories from the golden era of the post–World War II automotive industry. It was legend that a mom-and-pop tool-and-die shop might grow rich for years making one part required in thousands of cars. Who would have thought that Japanese and German automobile manufacturers would challenge the American car industry, putting hundreds of such shops out of work?

Ideal customers pay you well—eternally—with little effort. *Real* customers can be frustrating and elusive and require constant diligence.

The business owners who survive learn to apply their talents elsewhere. They acquire new skills and find customers in new markets.

How Different Are Potential Customers in Different Library Workplaces?

Independent consultants who are experienced with only one type of library in one locale often make the mistake of not researching how library workplaces differ. For example, you might have spent your entire career in public libraries and see yourself as a trailblazer in the realm of library-oriented emerging technologies. Then you bomb your first speech to a group of cutting-edge academic reference librarians, who considered your tech news old and tired. Your perceived arrogance will be gossip for weeks and affect your ability to land future contracts.

Researching your potential clients' habitat is a requirement at every stage of your new career, even if you have decades of experience with different types of libraries. Never take a client for granted. How an information professional in an international pharmaceutical company spends his or her time is different from a media specialist's workday in a rural school district. The scope and scale of the work are different. The vocabulary and tools are different. Their library users are different in age, education, and their types of requests.

The workplace culture might vary from suits and ties to blue jeans and t-shirts, strict hierarchical decision making to communal collaboration, and from decades of tradition to bleeding-edge innovation. Biochemists spend their days differently from schoolteachers and stay-at-home parents, as do the library employees who serve them. And searching for citations in PubMed is not the same as vetting K-6 educational software.

It also affects the very practical issue of how you get paid and how long it takes. A large public university, a suburban library district, a corporate marketing department, and a state legislature all have different styles of governance. Your payment might come from financial offices that are located in another state and requires reams of paperwork or from a small school district whose accounting system dates back to the Victorian era.

Don't be fooled by size either. It is gratifying, for example, when a personable

> Researching your potential clients' habitat is a requirement at every stage of your new career, even if you have decades of experience with different types of libraries. Never take a client for granted. How an information professional in an international pharmaceutical company spends his or her time is different from a media specialist's workday in a rural school district. The scope and scale of the work are different. The vocabulary and tools are different. Their library users are different in age, education, and their types of requests.

accounting specialist with the Department of Defense pays you from a credit card within 72 hours of your contract's completion, but you will wonder why that small Midwestern foundation took three months. "*Well, we skipped a monthly board meeting, and then Madge was on vacation, and then we lost the paperwork. Sorry.*"

The communities where your clients reside will affect the style by which decisions are made. In states like Wyoming, Kansas, Idaho, and Colorado, collaboration among libraries of all types is the norm, and finding partners for contracts is not difficult. In other states, it is possible to have in the same county a cluster of town or village libraries whose directors are forbidden from working together by their local public officials, despite the fact that the librarians themselves would be delighted to collaborate. Identifying those political minefields is part of the work of an independent consultant.

Finally, the differences among the operating styles of key political and financial decision makers within those libraries are perhaps the most important variables. If that key person is a change agent who is comfortable with making decisions quickly and taking action even quicker, it does not matter if they are a major in the Air Force managing the resources that support the base's library or the sole owner of a small publishing company interested in promoting its midlist to library acquisition committees. He or she will cut through the red tape to make things happen fast, which includes hiring you for your wise counsel.

What Works to Find and Reach Them, Regardless of Who They Are

Alexis de Tocqueville, in his iconic *Democracy in America* (1835), describes the reliance of Americans in 1831 on professional, trade, and service associations. Not much has changed since then.

Looking for an efficient way to connect with potential customers? Professional associations and trade and business organizations are universal in the library world. It's only a click away to uncover the Web sites for any type of library-related group, with detailed information about conferences, meetings, newsletter, blogs, classes, and after-hour meetups.

Many smaller, specialized associations and local chapters might not have a regularly maintained Web site. This leads to the second part of your mapping expedition: old-school word of mouth.

Ask. And ask again. Networking is more than pushing a brochure in someone's face or wheedling a signed contract. It is learning about who knows whom and building a bridge from where you are to where you want to be.

For example, the nice woman with whom you share a shuttle to the hotel tells you about the professional association she belongs to that hires local talent for breakfast speeches. You attend a meeting and engage the people at your table in conversations about their jobs and the other groups to which they belong. Those conversations lead you to a local conference, where you browse the exhibit hall and discover that the vendors are chatting about whose hiring because of a new grant for library leadership development. That's where you meet your next client, while discussing your work over a free cup of coffee.

What you will discover is that marketing your services is a constant dialogue. Sometimes it is a focused visit to a professional conference, and sometimes it is the casual conversation with a stranger while waiting in line at a busy grocery store. For more on the ins and outs of marketing see Crystal Schimpf's Chapter 6.

How Do They Fit into Your Strategic Plan and Business Model?

Generating leads is not enough.

Some territories charted on your map are richer than others, and it is important to keep in mind what you

> Generating leads is not enough.

need in order to succeed financially. You need to balance exploring untested opportunities, such as a consulting challenge that is larger than your previous contracts versus staying focused on profit and personal goals.

For example, you meet some great people who want to hire you for an international training contract. The folks are nice, the proposed program is definitely in your wheelhouse, and you know the contract will look great on the testimonials page of your Web site. Then you check with your bank and discover that the lovely touristy country that sounds so charming has restrictions on cash payments to foreigners. You will be paid in cheese and woven goods, which you will be expected to sell to a broker who typically takes 40 percent as a commission. This might work for big companies, but not for small potatoes such as you.

An example closer to home: The state capitol where the prospective client is located has no airport, and the fiscal agent does not reimburse for rental cars. The bus from the airport takes five hours and runs only twice a day. Is the inconvenience worth the fee?

Creating an online course sounds convenient, and you get to work at home in your pajamas. But if you have never created a multiweek course with interactive components on that particular platform, with that federally funded university's restrictions regarding images and captioning, you might end up working for $2.00 an hour by the time the contract is finished.

Assume there are many swamps and quicksand pits to tag on that map. Plan for hidden client expectations that might not be revealed in time for you to turn back unless you are willing to ask fiscal and legal questions at the beginning of your negotiations. See Melissa Stockton's Chapter 7 for more on contracts and when and how to say "no."

What Do Potential Customers Have in Common?

Regardless of type and size, there are factors that apply to any client—the kind of information you should be looking for in your first conversations. You will develop your own framework for what works best for you in terms of deciding if it is a good fit.

Tip: Don't rely only on what you read on their Web sites or in their brochures. The information might be out of date and might not apply to your specific clients or with the department or grant for which you are being considered. Always verify everything with the individual who is the point person for the contract in writing. It is a little embarrassing to apply for a project with a department that was shut down months ago or to call a library director whose business card you have been carrying around for months, only to discover that they were fired weeks before.

Who Makes Decisions?

One common red herring is to spend too much time courting someone who does not have the power to hire you or the influence to promote you successfully to the people who do. A typical scenario occurs when you are presenting at a conference of support staff—intelligent and engaged people who loved your workshop. Many stay to chat, and they discuss the problems in their libraries at length, praising your insights.

You exchange e-mails with them about your work and begin working toward feeling them out for a paying contract. Then you discover that although the members of your new fan club enjoyed chatting with you, they had no power to move from friendly conversation to a paying agreement. In fact, they might even be offended or annoyed when you bring up money.

Your challenge is to balance the time you take investing in your future client relationships and being a decent person who helps as you can against the reality of seeking work that pays the bills. Because there are so many sources of free and subsidized help for libraries, your new workplace friends justifiably might be confused, thinking you are able to volunteer your services because someone else is footing the costs.

Finding out who can and will make the decision to hire you will help you plan your calendar. A committee or board that meets monthly can drag decision making out ad infinitum, so don't count on a contract soon. If a conference committee is making the decision, do the individual members need to go back to their organizations in order to make a decision, or can they each act autonomously? Each level of approval can add weeks to closing on a contract.

Life would simpler if a decision always meant a "yes or no" with a figure and date attached. Much more frustrating is if you learn that the group also believes it has the right to micromanage every detail, even after you have made the important decisions with the representative whom you thought had the authority to seal the deal.

So, again, the advice is assume nothing, and stay curious.

Who Pays the Bill?

> Tip: Most fiscal agents follow formal protocol, which translates into a 30-day billing cycle. Being paid in advance or on the day a project is finished is the exception, not the rule. The same is true regarding reimbursement for expenses, such as travel. So, in managing your cash flow, you can always ask the client for payment in advance, but don't assume that they have the ability to pay anything ahead of time.

You will have to deal with at least three different payment scenarios:

The Larger Organization

The most common way to be paid is by the organization in which the library resides: the school district, the local government agency, the institution of higher learning, or the agency or institution. In effect, you will have two negotiations with two sets of people and politics. Although the client who hires you probably will help you take care of the paperwork, it's a good idea to find out who issues purchase orders and approves your check. If something goes wrong, it also is good to know whom to contact. In fact, touching base with them before there is a problem is preferable; this makes it easier when you have to hunt down a delayed or lost payment.

Third Party

Because budgets are tight and libraries often are under a magnifying glass regarding how they are spending their money, hiring an independent consultant such as you can be viewed as a luxury by paid and volunteer watchdogs alike. Consequently, many libraries use third-party sources of money. It might be a community foundation with funds pledged to support technological development, a state grant for library board training, or a friendly vendor who will underwrite your conference program. Make sure you know potential restrictions upfront. Do they need you to fold all of your expenses into one fee? Do they have a cap on motel or airfare? Are they required to pay the money to an individual and not to your business corporation?

The Organization Itself

Sometimes, the library client itself will be paying your fee, either because they are in charge of their budget with no second-party fiscal agent (they don't have to ask permission for the institution where they are embedded) or because they are autonomous (separate money). Examples include library districts (a specific way of creating a library service organization as its own taxing entity mandated by state government) and libraries organized as non-profit organizations. However, there still might be state- and federal-level parameters as to how they spend their funds. For more details on finance in your new business, see Denise Shockley's Chapter 4.

What Might They Need and Want?

Some potential clients want you to show up and solve their problems without their having to change anything they are doing. Some expect you to roll up your sleeves and get to work. Others will want you to look over their shoulders and comment.

For example, two library agencies want you to review their curriculum and make suggestions for improvement. The first client is easy to work with, meaning you seem to be on the same page, they are pleased with the work that you do, and you see them apply some of the ideas immediately.

However, although the two contracts appeared identical, you never connect successfully with the second client. The big clue, which perhaps you refused to acknowledge, is that even after three meetings they were questioning your proposal and requesting a total different approach. Each time you said you were not the right person, they insisted you were, and then you started again. Your mistake was to assume that what had worked so well with the first client would fit the needs of the second client.

> Tip: Success can make you smug. Even if the needs of the clients are familiar to you, assume that they are unique, and avoid shortcuts when deciding how to approach their situation.

The Person Who Hires You versus the People You Work With

Sometimes, particularly in professional coaching relationships, you communicate and work with only one person throughout the lifetime of a contract. The individual who contacts you at the beginning of the process is the same person with whom you discuss goals, timelines, and budgets; who gives you feedback about your proposal; and with whom you interact during the course of the agreement. That same person evaluates you, pays you, and provides you with follow-up as to the lasting impact of your efforts.

Most of the time, however, particularly if you're signing on as a trainer or consultant, you'll have two distinct entities to please: the person or group that hires and pays you and the people who make up the audience or team with whom you will work. This duality can occur if you have been hired to critique, improve, or modify the work of current employees.

Never assume that the people who hired you have told your prospective audience or team the full story regarding your presence. It is up to you to find out if the person who hired you told the people who are waiting for you on the other side of the door:

- Who you are, your credentials, and background
- Why the institution or individual hired you
- The scope and scale of your proposed contract
- Your legitimate authority to supervise, order work and supplies, make decisions, and execute changes

Ironically, the person who hired you might think your presence is a reward for good behavior, whereas attendees or team members assume your program or intervention is a punishment replete with hidden messages of wrongdoing. And sometimes, the attendees and team members are right, and you are the last to know.

The better scenario is when, early on in the contracting process, your client solicits input from the proposed audience, whether for a staff day presentation or working side by side with employees and volunteers to upgrade the library's technology. Asking for input might include sending out a survey, requesting a list of concerns, or participating in planning meetings. If they don't normally do this, you should feel free to supply a survey for them to share as part of your contract. It only enhances your presentation, training, or project.

You might find yourself in a situation where there is an ongoing conflict between different factions in the library, and your presence is being used to support one side or another. If you find yourself confronted in a meeting or public arena by people questioning your motives, the best response is to tell the truth and stick to the parameters of your contract.

Tip: When challenged or tempted to take sides, remember that you were asked to do a job and, for legal and financial reasons, you intend to finish that contract. Anything else is none of your business.

What should you do when someone invokes the union and/or employee organization's contracts as a reason the actions you suggest cannot be implemented?

One reason that outsider consultants can instigate change is because they take nothing for granted. So, if someone says that the union, or state law, or an obscure contract with the school district, or a sponsoring organization proclaims something is forbidden, the consultant will ask the magic question:

How do you know that is true?

The conscientious independent consultant will do what's necessary to answer the question, from asking to see the contract in question, calling for a meeting with the legal department of the university, inviting the district attorney to comment, bringing up the URL that lists the legislation under that state's collection of library-related laws, or requesting that the state attorney general's office provide a ruling.

A good consultant does not mind being the ignorant person in the meeting who asks obvious and even annoying questions and requests a copy of the document that everyone else takes for granted. Your questions can uncover new information that points to success for your customer.

Venues, Good and Bad

In the computer age, the location from where you conduct your work for your client can be a physical location, virtual space, or a combination of both. And regardless of how smart, experienced, and accommodating your client is, the first time you enter the room they set aside for your facilitation or log into the webinar platform where you are expected to present can be a surprise.

> Assume everything and anything can and will go wrong, and prepare for alternatives. Be flexible. The better you are able to stay good humored and constructive, the more likely the client will want you back. You have the power and influence to make glitches a better experience for everyone.

Assume everything and anything can and will go wrong, and prepare for alternatives. Be flexible. The better you are able to stay good humored and constructive, the more likely the client will want you back. You have the power and influence to make glitches a better experience for everyone.

For online programs, test the software the day before the program, even if you have utilized it for months on behalf of other clients. Unannounced upgrades can make your system inoperable overnight, which will be the day you are broadcasting to a national audience.

In addition, old-school backup plans are a good idea:

- Does the room where you will be broadcasting into have a landline so the client can switch to a speakerphone in case the online audio speakers fail?
- Do you have paper versions of your slides available in case your visual access cuts out during a multisite presentation?
- Do your slides and material reside within multiple computers controlled by your client and his or her producers in case your system fails?

For live programs, have you sent your client, and everyone else who might be involved in setting up for your visit, one e-mail that lists all of your requirements? You'll send this even if your client asked you to fill out an elaborate questionnaire beforehand. Maybe you also will review the requirements one more time in that last conference call before you board your plane.

When you are physically at the site, your first job is to seek out the technical support staff at the hotel or conference center or library meeting room, thank them profusely and sincerely for their help, and make them your new best friends. And then, you will double-check the sight lines from where you will presenting from every seat and table, as well as test the technology, both audio and visual, check the charge on the batteries, and ensure the lighting is adjustable, including lowering curtains to keep out the blinding sun in the morning.

PART TWO: THE CUSTOMER

Now that you have a sketch of your marketing map and know what to expect from your customers in general terms, you can explore specific characteristics of individual and organizational library customers.

Individual Customers

If your career as an independent consultant revolves around professional coaching, training, and mentoring, most of your clients will be individuals. You also might be selling individuals a product, such as e-books, individual seats to webinars and online courses, memberships, and subscriptions that pay for access to events and publications.

The best way to find these individual customers is by becoming active with your local professional library association. You might also branch out to regional and national associations by volunteering, serving on committees, and offering free programs, in person and online, to audition for new audiences and to build a reputation.

Some people are addicted to continuing education opportunities; they are an example of the uncommon ideal customer. They see education as an investment and often become your regulars at conferences and online programs if they like your style.

However, more typical are the individuals who will want your services and products because they are experiencing some kind of professional change. They include job hunters and "career shifters" wanting to upgrade workplace skills, people preparing for a new job, and retirees who want to keep up with changes in the library profession as well as connect with old friends at conferences. You will also encounter library school undergraduate and graduate students looking to earn extra credit or supplement classroom learning.

A special category includes the people who need verifiable continuing education units (CEUs) to maintain certification for their current jobs and future careers. These potential customers might work for a library employer who requires that they seek CEUs, but doesn't supply opportunities during their workday. Or their state might require licensing requirements for degreed library professionals that must be updated every few years.

To capture their interest and dollars, you'll need to partner with an agency that provides accreditation services or find a library school willing to vouch for you. The simplest path is to start by contacting your state library and asking what is needed for your online and live presentations to be approved for CE credits and to have that approval guaranteed in writing.

> Tip: Individual customers are often paying for your services and products out of their own pockets or are getting a reimbursement from their employer. You will need to decide how much cash credit you'll extend to them and if it's worth pursuing them legally if the payment never arrives or a check bounces.

The biggest financial issue challenging a library-oriented business built on individual customers (versus being hired by library agencies) will be how much money you make per transaction, given the time it takes to manage each customer.

For example, if you are selling 50 individual seats for a webinar at $50 each, $2,500 sounds like a decent amount of gross profit. However, consider how much time you will have to spend with each person or agency that signs up, from answering questions about the content beforehand, to arranging for payment from their employer or financial office, to handling technical problems during the webcast, to dealing with certificates of participation and CEUs afterward. The hourly net profit for $2,500 from a single institutional organization can be far more than $2,500 garnered from managing relationships with 50 individuals.

Library Institutions

If you are like most library consultants, the majority of your customers will be libraries and related institutions, including library conferences, library associations, state libraries and regional systems, and service and membership consortia.

> Tip: The landscape is constantly changing, so the best approach is to do your own research, which means contacting institutions via e-mail or phone to verify facts you capture online. Do not make important decisions based only on what you learn from Web sites and social media; talk to a human being directly!

As this is being written, a new wave of retirements is sweeping through library institutions. New leadership means new interpretations of long-standing rules and new opportunities for training or consulting. For the independent consultant, change means that it can take some digging to find out who actually controls the funds and makes decisions about whom to hire.

Libraries fall into five main categories, with variations depending on state law, custom, and local culture. Different states use different names for the same configurations, such as networks, cooperatives, and consortia, and the same names for different configurations, such as systems and districts. So never assume you know what your clients mean by a designation. Ask, and ask again.

Public Libraries

Public libraries can be structured by state law to fall under the control of local government, such as municipal or county libraries, as standalone districts, or as independent nonprofit corporations, which receive the bulk of their funding through contracts with local government. Some monies come from individuals, local foundations, Friends groups, and state and federal funding agencies.

Funding organizations work from the priorities set in their strategic plans, which are the agreements they have with their stakeholders regarding how they plan to donate their money. One year they might focus on the needs of children and new Americans. The next year, it will be about information literacy and economic development in rural areas. The next might involve community outreach and boosting educational achievement for secondary students. The more you align your work with those goals, the more likely you will find opportunities to partner with clients.

Public libraries are governed by elected or appointed boards, including city councils, county commissioners, and independent library boards.

Not all library boards have the same authority over their libraries. A library board can be a governing board, which means it can make legal and financial decisions, including hiring and firing the director, approving the budget, and establishing library policies. A governing board has the final say.

An advisory board, on the other hand, makes suggestions to the governing board. Some advisory boards have strong support from the community and are respected by the elected officials, so their suggestions have the same authority as if they came from a governing board. However, in other cases, the advisory board is relegated to a minor voice in the operation of the library.

Tip: In many cases, the governing board will approve hiring you, not the director. You might learn that you have been spending weeks talking to people who have no say over the budget or your contract, and the process will start from scratch after the director informs the governing board of their intention to hire you.

The structure of library districts is mandated by their state's laws. Districts often fall along the borders of counties but are separate from county government and governed by their own library boards. Their funds come from their own taxing district; in some states, these are called special districts.

Individual public libraries also might be part of a system (which is another loose term that can mean just about anything collaborative) or a district. Each individual library has a certain level of autonomy, with its own board, and the larger district or system also has an overarching board.

When you are working for a public library, regardless of its legal and financial model, you are working for local government. You might find that working for the public library means that you'll also be working for the town manager, city manager, or county human resources department. It explains why your first day on the contract could be spent visiting the offices of elected officials and explaining what you are doing and why to people you've never heard of before but who have the power to cancel your contract.

Learn about the community the public library serves: its history, citizens, economy, and current challenges. That way, you will be prepared when your library clients keep talking about "the lawsuit" or some other current challenge.

Academic Libraries

Academic libraries serve higher education, referring to educational institutions that students attend after high school. They range from high-tech information centers in vocational schools to historic buildings on the campuses of Ivy League universities. Large universities often have multiple libraries with unique collections and subject matter specialists. Medical, law, and engineering schools usually have their own libraries.

When you are working for an academic library, you are working for the larger institution as well. The library's strategic plan, for example, is a subset of the academic institution's plan. The library's culture is part of the larger institution's culture. Although they may receive only a small percentage of their funding from state and federal governments, state universities must comply with certain regulations and protocols from those entities.

As with public libraries and their relationship with the communities they serve, research the larger learning institution—its history, its mission, the student body, and the focus and strengths of the curriculum. Is the institution prouder of their world-class philosophy department or the school of veterinary medicine? Is your potential community college library client one that is part of an organization dedicated to providing a welcoming environment for new Americans and older students with jobs and families? Are they invested in distance learning and continuing education? Knowing their focus gives you an edge when working with them as clients.

Special Libraries

Special libraries, the most diverse category of libraries, serve the specialized needs of institutions in the government, nonprofit, and private sectors.

Special libraries are more likely to employ people who are subject specialists (often with multiple graduate degrees), rather than those with library school degrees, and their job titles are less likely to be that of "librarian." (This is important in case you are making reasonable—and wrong—decisions about who is in charge and who has the power to sign a check.) A special library's reference personnel are more likely to hold graduate degrees in fields other than library science and most likely serve other degreed professionals, from accountants to zoologists.

Government special libraries include those that support rocket scientists at NASA, judges and lawyers at county courts, wildlife biologists in national parks, military intelligence officers within the Department of Defense, and geologists at state-funded engineering schools.

Nonprofit special libraries include patient information centers in community hospitals; research libraries accessible to students, scholars, and the general public in big-city botanical and art museums; archives in trade and professional associations; and self-published genealogical records shelved in local history societies.

In the business world, most major corporations have their own research libraries, whether they make their money in banking, cosmetics, computers, agriculture, or mining.

Independent consultants conduct two general categories of work for special libraries: those that require expert knowledge of the library's area of specialization, such as facilitating a class in medical terminology to aid in searching health-oriented databases, and those that apply to most library organizations, such as basic project management and supervision.

In either event, most special libraries dwell within a larger institution with its own set of rules. Learn about that institution: whom the special library serves; the library's collections, services, and staffing; and its own strategic focus. For example, is it a medical library with an emphasis on embedding its staff in clinical meetings and providing downloads of key documents to mobile devices so that emergency room professional staff have diagnostic tools? Or a law library that supports the collaborative atmosphere of the legal firm so that the library hosts a large "salon" where comfy couches invite people to stay and talk about long-term, theoretical issues?

At the very least, consulting for special libraries means immersing yourself in a new vocabulary and culture. Part of the pleasure of working with special libraries lies in browsing collections and learning from experts about practical applications of plant pathology, Egyptology, the history of children's book illustrations, the Resistance in Germany against Hitler in World War II, and the book arts.

School Libraries

School libraries, often called media centers, can be found serving preschools through senior high, which is the traditional K-12 designation. In this age of digital learning many school libraries are the center of technology, and school librarians help students learn how to evaluate information. According to the *State of America's Libraries Report 2017*, school libraries currently face the challenges of "fake news," rising intolerance, and funding.

The people who run them could be certified professional teacher-librarians with multiple college degrees or part-time clerks or even volunteers whose tasks are limited to processing, shelving, and checking out books. In some schools, the library staff members are considered part of the teaching staff, and the school library is considered central to student success. In others, the library is considered an outdated luxury. School librarians work within the curriculum of the school and, ideally, partner with other teachers to support and even enhance the students' learning experience.

Most of the time, outside of the richest communities, wealthy private schools, and largest school districts, an individual school library doesn't have the funds or staff to warrant hiring an outside consultant. Instead, you'll be contracted at the school district's administrative level to serve many school libraries. Depending on the size of the school district, you might be hired by the school district's media coordinator, who oversees all of the school libraries, or the human resources department, the superintendent of schools, or even the school board.

Tip: The layers of bureaucracy and regulations, up to and including at the national level, make it difficult to land long-term contracts in school districts without the appropriate education-based credentials and testimonials to satisfy school administrators. Find out what is required before you assume you will have a reasonable chance of making a sale.

The National Center for Education Statistics reports that 90 percent of traditional public schools have a library, whereas only 49 percent of public charter schools have a library.

Joint-Use Libraries

Joint-use libraries merge different types of libraries or libraries with other agencies, sharing physical space, technology, staff, collections, programming, etc., on a permanent basis.

Sometimes, the only reason the different agencies are combined is to save money. The organizers of the mergers, often elected and appointed officials, might not realize that the different institutions have incompatible missions, policies, and staffing requirements. The different institutions even may have different pay scales, job descriptions, and procedures for the same positions. And what if it is not clear who has supervisory authority over a department or individual staffer? The outside consultant can be walking a political tightrope if the different libraries are not working together in harmony. Which library or agency has hired you? And how does the other side feel about your contract?

Typical pairings include:

The school library and public library combination, which often is housed in the school, sometimes with different entrances. In some cases the public library is only "activated" when school lets out, and the "adult" section is inaccessible to students except during evening and weekend hours.

The public library and academic library duo, which shares its own unique building. One interesting conflict is the differences between how a college reference librarian and a public library reference librarian might respond to a question from a student. The college librarian would want to teach the student how to conduct the research themselves, whereas the public librarian will likely find the source and may even provide the answer. Reconciling those two approaches does not happen instantly; figuring out the reference policy is one example of dozens of negotiations that need to happen for the sake of a smoothly running institutional marriage.

The library (public or academic) and the museum, community center, theater space, public health organization, or civic center. Sometimes they just share physical space; other times, they will share staff and services. The public library might host a privately funded museum within its walls, or the art gallery or theater might be attached to the library physically, but with a separate identity in the community.

Joint-use libraries offer more opportunities to build your reputation beyond the limits of one kind of library. The challenge is negotiating the politics and cultures of the merged organizations—sometimes tied together with little in common besides a physical location and a shared name.

As libraries evolve new services and relationships with other agencies, these old categories might change, so keep alert for new trends.

Conferences

Some library consultants can make money doing keynotes or preconferences at state, regional, and national trade and professional conferences and conventions. Although the words are used interchangeably, conventions tend to be more about the exhibits, and conferences are more about the discussions and educational opportunities, including seminars and workshops.

These opportunities usually come later in your career once you have a written a book, built a reputation in your field while gainfully employed, established yourself as an expert on a popular topic, or established yourself as a "thought leader" with new and invigorating ideas.

Conferences and conventions can fall into three categories: First are those that are specific to an established organization and that are produced on a regular calendar, usually annually. This category includes most of the conferences and conventions held by library associations or those sponsored by specific software or sponsored hardware vendors for their customers as user group gatherings. Examples include the American Library Association (ALA), Public Library Association (PLA), Association of College and Research Libraries (ACRL), and state and regional offshoots of these organizations.

> Tip: Be aware that most of the associations start planning their conferences a year or more in advance. So the timeline for communicating with the organizers is measured in years, not weeks. You will need to stay up to date regarding who will be making programming decisions and educating them in terms of what you have to offer their event. The good news is that cancellations are not uncommon, and you might be asked at the last minute to fill in. So even if you are turned down, stay positive, and stay in touch.

Second are conferences that are launched by an independent group of like-minded people who join together solely for creating the conference, which may be intended as a one-shot event. These conferences often are about topical issues and provide cutting-edge information. They can be fueled by a desire to create an event that caters to people with their particular interests.

The library community's calendar is replete with smaller specialized tech conferences and other library conferences devoted to topics such as interlibrary loans, marketing, and the future of libraries.

The third conferences are those that are put together by a coalition of associations, vendors, state libraries, and sponsoring libraries. For example, such a conference might be organized by a group of public library children's librarians, school librarians, and others in education, such as teachers and specialists (Ed.S.), and funded by library associations and state libraries.

The organizers share an interest in the latest discoveries around the development of the brain in ages 5 years to 18 years. Or it might be a group of library associations that share a geographical region and meet to bring together librarians and library workers across state lines.

These associations are broad in scope and often attract innovators and leaders; they are fertile grounds for finding clients that will teach you as much as they learn from you.

> Tip: Most professional library conferences are sponsored by membership associations and often have policies that forbid paying members for services—specifically for their services at association conventions. Consequently, many library consultants will drop their memberships in their professional associations and find other ways to support the organizations through donations of time and money.

Many professional associations require presenters to pay for registering for conferences, even for those meetings where they are volunteering their services. This practice is most common in the academic world, where those fees are paid for by institutional employers.

Unless you are planning both to donate your services and to pay for attending, make sure your contract clearly states details about money. Don't assume, and don't accept a verbal assurance that the rules don't apply to you. Few events in the life of an independent consultant are more frustrating than showing up for an event to present and being handed an invoice rather than a check.

Because conferences and conventions bring together hundreds, or even thousands, of people, you'll need to plan how you'll use your time and resources to connect with potential paying customers. Do you want to buy ads in the print program or a banner in the lobby of the hotel? Rent a booth? Serve on a committee? Create a brochure? Volunteer behind the scenes or at a help desk? Sponsor the food at a welcoming event? Or volunteer to facilitate a strategic planning meeting? Or present a program for free?

Over time, you will learn what works best for you, both in terms of your contribution to your customers and colleagues, as well as providing you with connections to paying customers. Be ruthless about evaluating both short-term and long-term financial benefits. If you find that you aren't booking contracts that can be traced back to conference participation, you may need to rethink this aspect of your marketing strategies.

Library Support and Membership Organizations

Outside of the libraries are arrayed overlapping layers of agencies, associations, and consortia. Traditionally, they are where most libraries receive educational and technological support. They include national library associations, regional associations (both interstate and intrastate), state libraries and regional systems, and library consortia.

National library associations are membership organizations that provide live and virtual conferences, educational programs, books and certification programs, venues for publishing research papers, and support and guidance for the library profession in the form of research, white papers, and commentary on national issues.

Some are focused on specific library audiences, such as children and those library users who live in institutions, such as prisons and hospitals. Others are organized around topics, such as expertise in the arts, medicine, law, or theology. Some focus on librarians that share demographics, such as ethnicity or living in and serving rural areas. Examples include the Association for Rural and Small Libraries annual conference or the Substance Abuse Librarians & Information Specialists (SALIS) and Association of Mental Health Librarians (AMHL) joint conference.

The associations that have a specific focus are likely to foster statewide affiliates and statewide and regional chapters. Although an individual library in a law firm, medical school, or art museum might not have funds to hire an independent consultant or trainer, a regional chapter meeting can bring together staff from dozens of special libraries. The chapters often collaborate, so if you do well with one, don't be surprised if you are invited to speak at others.

State libraries are established by state law and, with the exception of the agency in Hawaii, have little oversight over the day-to-day operations of libraries in their state. Their purposes range from managing historical archives, to providing research services for state employees, to staffing browsing collections specific to the state's culture and history, to negotiating discounts for databases, to funding consultants to support library success.

Each state library receives funds through federal and state government grants and other funding organizations that are earmarked for different types of projects. The discretionary funds for hiring independent consultants often come from these grants. The strategic plans for state libraries, which are posted online, will give you a good idea of what initiatives they intend to fund so you can align your services to their goals.

Interstate regional library associations form across areas that share cultural and regional identities, including New England, the Southeast, the Rocky Mountain West and the adjacent Plains States, and the Pacific Northwest. Members tend to like the smaller conferences and the sense of shared identity.

Intrastate regional associations, which are called systems, networks, and cooperatives, were common up to the early part of the 21st century. They were created mostly as independent nonprofits or as extensions of the state libraries in the 1960s and 1970s. Originally they were established to support union catalogs, where libraries would share information about their collections in massive rows of card catalogs, duplicating author, title, and subject cards for dozens and even hundreds of libraries. They also provided cataloging services for smaller libraries. As library technology evolved, the regional systems focused more on shared technical services, including maintaining computer servers for managing collections, e-mail, and Web sites.

The systems also manage courier services among their member libraries to support interlibrary loan—physically moving books from place to place through the mail and networks of delivery services. In regions where libraries make their physical collections available to each other's library users, the courier service is the foundation for ensuring books borrowed from one library and returned to a different library find their way home again.

These regional systems offer training and educational services that meet local needs, especially for smaller and underfinanced libraries, helping to equalize disparities in funding between urban and rural parts of their state. They have been a major employer of independent consultants for cataloging, consulting, and training.

However, shrinking budgets have forced the merger and elimination of many of these regional systems in all but a very few states. A common scenario is for a new organization, sometimes called a "super-system," to emerge, which handles statewide courier and technology services.

On one hand, these organizations—the library associations, the state libraries, and the regional systems—are your biggest competitors. Supported by tax money and grants, they likely will offer the same services you offer to the same library institutions and individuals at no charge.

On the other hand, they can be your biggest supporters and allies. If they like your work and receive good feedback from their library clients, they might partner with you for both short-term and long-term contracts and recommend you for consulting and training contracts.

As said before, every state and every institution have a different model for doing business, and key personnel are always changing. Consequently, making and sustaining working relationships with the personnel of these groups should be the most important marketing strategy.

Applying Your Skills Outside of the Library Community

Because of referrals from your pleased library customers, you may find opportunities with clients outside of the library community. All workplaces tend to have similar soft skill issues regarding project management, customer service, supervision, planning, etc. Specific library skills, such as research and organizing data, are applicable in any organization. However, some cultural differences can make or break your next referral outside of libraries.

Here are some generalizations regarding how other workplaces might differ from typical libraries.

Tip: Fifty percent of adjusting to a different workplace's culture is learning the vocabulary. Read through their Web sites, find a couple of friendly mentors to interview, and if possible, attend a luncheon meeting or visit their exhibit hall at a trade convention.

Public Sector

From municipal zoning boards to federal agencies, government agencies tend to be limited as to what they can do, and decisions take longer. Long-timers memorize a litany of rules and regulations that must be obeyed, even if they contradict each other, but experienced employees also are skilled at workarounds. Find out what the constraints are during your first meeting.

Payment processes usually are more involved, with multiple forms and sticky requirements. For example, does your small-business corporation have a Dun & Bradstreet (D&B) D-U-N-S Number or accept American Express cards for payment? These might be required if you are working for certain federal agencies. Have you filled out the 28-page contract from that state agency, promising in a notarized form you won't interfere with elections in that state? That form that was hidden on page 24?

Tip: Lots of details are required to satisfy government financial officers—triple-check anything you submit.

Private Sector

On the other hand, unless you plan to work for major corporations, which tend to operate at the same speed as large federal agencies, the business world, even small mom-and-pop shops, is more likely to be interested in fast results. They have a sense of urgency sometimes lacking in the other two main sectors.

Businesses are less likely to operate from one guaranteed income source, meaning their cash flow can be erratic, so it is less likely their money can be encumbered to pay you. This means it is more likely that they will call with the bad news that they can't afford to hire you this time . . . maybe next year.

Because of the diversity of business types and models, it is crucial to learn about their industry. State and national trade associations are good places to start, as well as finding people who can get you up to speed quickly. Ask lots of questions; most businesspeople love to talk about their work.

The good news? Most business owners and administrators can make hiring decisions quickly, and there is less red tape when it comes to payment.

The bad news? Most businesspeople don't make time for working with consultants, so unless you are an accountant or lawyer, they are less likely to seek your help.

Nonprofit Sector

Charities and other nonprofit organizations operate from donations and grants. Like public-sector and private-sector agencies, they each are a part of a specific cohort, be it a religious or secular community, and you should not make assumptions about what they care about.

The hardest nonprofit issue is what some people label the "poverty mentality" that can pervade even the richest nonprofit organization. Consequently, in the nicest way you can, ask in the first conversation about finances; there is a good chance they expect you to donate your services and might not bring it up until you ask about budgets and payments.

One strategy is to create specific services that you can offer to nonprofit organizations for a discount, perhaps during those times when you are less busy—for example, a stripped-down version of strategic planning or a generic webinar that has the same information as your more elaborate slideshows but with fewer illustrations.

Research is the key to venturing outside the borders of your library marketing map. It is not just about facts and figures; success is tied to understanding the mind-set of people who work in different organizations and industries.

CONCLUSION

Every independent library consultant creates a marketplace map unique to their circumstances: their talents, their personalities, their goals, and the times and places from which they run their consulting business.

The most common business failures are caused by smugness and complacency, particularly if there is a major shift in society, culture, or technology. The most successful consultants will create an interactive map, which is constantly responding to the changes their customers are experiencing.

Consider this review of the marketplace map a starting point. Bon voyage.

RESOURCES

American Library Association, *State of America's Libraries Report 2017* http://www.ala.org/news/state-americas-libraries-report-2017/school-libraries

National Center for Education Statistics. *Characteristics of Public and Private Elementary and Secondary Schools in the United States: Results from the 2011–2012 Schools and Staffing Survey.* https://nces.ed.gov/pubs2013/2013312.pdf

Tocqueville, Alexis de, *Democracy in America.* https://www.gutenberg.org/files/815/815-h/815-h.htm

FURTHER READING

Campbell, Clark A. *The New One-Page Project Manager: Communicate and Manage Any Project with a Single Sheet of Paper.* 2nd edition, Wiley, 2012.

Gastil, John. *Democracy in Small Groups: Participation, Decision Making & Communication.* 2nd edition, Efficacy Press, 2014.

Gerber, Michael E. *The E-Myth Series: The E-Myth Revisited: Why Most Small Businesses Don't Work and What to Do about It.* HarperCollins, 1995.

Goldratt, Eliyahu and Jeff Cox. *The Goal: A Process of Ongoing Improvement.* 2nd revised edition, North River Press, 1992.

Grote, Dick. *Discipline Without Punishment: The Proven Strategy That Turns Problem Employees into Superior Performers.* 2nd edition, AMACOM, 2006.

Kendrick, Tom. *Results Without Authority: Controlling a Project When the Team Doesn't Report to You.* 2nd edition, AMACOM, 2012.

Kremer, Chuck, Ron Rizzuto, and John Cash. *Managing by the Numbers: A Commonsense Guide to Understanding And Using Your Company's Financials.* Basic Books, 2000.

McKenna, Patrick J. and David H. Maister. *First Among Equals: How to Manage a Group of Professionals.* Free Press, 2005.

Mosvick, Roger K. and Robert B. Nelson. *We've Got to Start Meeting Like This: A Guide to Successful Meeting Management.* 2nd revised edition, Park Avenue Productions, 1996.

Portney, Stanley. *Project Management for Dummies.* 4th edition, Wiley, 2013.

Raines, Claire and Lara Ewing. *The Art of Connecting: How to Overcome Differences, Build Rapport, and Communicate Effectively with Anyone.* AMACOM, 2006.

Ryan, Rob. *Smartups: Lessons from Rob Ryan's Entrepreneur America Boot Camp for Start-Ups.* Cornell University Press, 2002.

Verzuh, Eric. *The Fast Forward MBA in Project Management: Quick Tips, Speedy Solutions, and Cutting-Edge Ideas.* Wiley, 1999.

4

Know the Numbers That Tell Your Story: The Legal and Financial Aspects of Your New Business

Denise Shockley, Independent Consultant

Information specialists developing their own consulting business have many legal and financial decisions to consider. Assessing these options early on will assist you in determining the best choices for your unique business needs. From choosing a business structure to developing contracts, forming a clear business plan enables you to monitor the health of your business and achieve goals that you want to achieve.

Legal and financial implications for information professional consultants may seem like considerations to be determined after your consulting business has been developed. However, choosing a business structure and assessing potential tax implications are critical to financial success. These implications can affect all other areas of your business planning and future success.

This chapter explores various aspects of these legal and financial decisions. First, it discusses the importance and key elements of developing of a business plan, through in-depth review of the various types of business structures, looking at the various types of business entities and potential implications for choosing each structure. Second, the tax implications to consider for each type of business entity are explored. Lastly, bookkeeping and accounting considerations from business startup, to tax planning, ongoing financial planning, and business growth are addressed.

DEVELOPING A BUSINESS PLAN

Taking the time to develop a business plan will help you map out your goals, opportunities, and strategies. It provides a guide for making initial legal and financial decisions. Rather than thinking about producing a traditional document, the first step is developing a strategy that provides clarity about your work, your processes, and your impact.

Seth Godin's "Modern Business Plan" (http://sethgodin.typepad.com/seths_blog/2010/05/the-modern-business-plan.html) is an excellent place to start in the business planning process to develop clarity about your foundation and strategy. He suggests the following five sections:

- Truth—Describing the world as it is, needs, competitors, successes, failures (market analysis)
- Assertions—What will you change? For whom? (mission, vision, values)
- Alternatives—Flexibility to adjust when the assertions are incorrect (processes, vision)
- People—Who will you work with? How will you work with them? (strategy, vision)
- Money—How much will you need? Expected cash flow, costs, financial statements (bookkeeping, accounting)

If you decide to develop a more traditional plan, there are a plethora of options, including templates that you can use to guide the process. The key steps in any business planning process will include the following: write it down, keep it simple, be specific, and get feedback. Whether you work with a mentor, colleague, or friend, getting constructive feedback can be one of the most valuable investments in creating a successful business plan. There are also consultants who specialize in this area and can provide insight into the process as well as providing valuable feedback.

CHOOSING A BUSINESS STRUCTURE

Choosing a business structure is a critical first step after developing a business plan. Businesses structures, and in particular, business entities, are simply legal structures that are necessary for financial and tax purposes. Business structures vary, and each type has its own benefits and drawbacks in different business scenarios. Specific business entities will directly affect your liability, paperwork, and taxes required as a business owner.

To choose the best business structure for your particular needs, it is important to choose a business entity type that best represents the type of business you are forming. *Business entities* are specific business structures. There are several business entity types, and each varies depending on whether you are operating as a single-person business or one with partners. Understanding each of these as potential options as a consultant will aid you in selecting the option that works best for you.

The key principle when choosing a business entity is simplicity. Although there are financial and monetary implications for each type of business entity, choosing one does not require you to be a "numbers person." It is important to note, though, that if you do not understand the basics of a particular business entity type, it is probably not the right fit for you and your business needs. Some business entity types are more complex than others, and gaining insight into each of these is helpful in choosing a business structure that makes the most sense for your business and individual circumstances. Business entity types and options can be fluid, and a business owner may find that there is a necessity to change as their business grows.

The most common business entity types include sole proprietorships, partnerships, corporations, and limited liability companies (LLC). We will explore each of these business entity types in depth, including liability, paperwork, and tax requirements for each specific business entity type, along with general information about the entity type itself.

Sole Proprietorship

A sole proprietorship is the simplest and most common business entity type, and is probably the business entity type that most new independent solo contractors choose when considering their business structure, offering complete control and being easy to form. A sole proprietorship is not a separate legal entity, and therefore has no additional legal business requirements; however, it is important to note that those who choose a sole proprietorship will be responsible for all legal and financial liabilities as owners of the business.

Owners of a sole proprietorship can operate under their own personal name or a trade name. Those with trade names are not required to create separate bank accounts under that name, and those with sole proprietorships can legally make financial transactions in their personal name. However, as you will see in the bookkeeping section of this chapter, comingling can make financial and tax recordkeeping both more complex and vulnerable to errors and inconsistencies.

Because of the simplicity of a sole proprietorship and ease with which a business owner can operate financially without additional paperwork, sole proprietors often find themselves comingling their personal and business affairs. This is a unique feature of this business entity, as other entities such as an LLC do not allow such mingling. Because the lines of business and personal can blur, it is important for the business owner to keep good records, particularly so that they are sufficient for tax purposes and comply with federal requirements for recordkeeping for a sole proprietorship.

Taxes for business owners of a sole proprietorship are fairly straightforward. The business owner simply reports any profit or loss from their business on their personal income tax return on Form 1040, Schedule C. The "bottom line," or final numbers from Schedule C, then transfers to your personal tax return (Form 1040). Note that if you are an owner of a sole proprietorship, you are responsible for paying all applicable taxes, including self-employment and estimated taxes, when appropriate.

Many businesses often begin as sole proprietorships and eventually transition to more complex business entities, depending on the business's growth and needs. However, that is not to say anyone who owns a sole proprietorship ever needs to migrate to another business entity type. Sole proprietorships can be extremely useful and beneficial for individuals, especially in the case of single business owners, and for the purposes of this book, information specialist consultants.

Quick Facts about Sole Proprietorship:

- **Liability**—The business owner is personally liable for all financial and legal obligations.
- **Paperwork**—Every sole proprietor is required to keep sufficient records to comply with federal tax requirements regarding business records; however, no additional recordkeeping is required.
- **Taxes**—The business owner reports profit or loss from the business on their personal income tax return, Form 1040, Schedule C.

Partnership

Partnerships are a legal relationship between two or more people for a single business. Each partner contributes money, property, or labor and shares in the profits and losses. Because this type of business entity involves multiple individuals who share the decision-making responsibility, it is important to understand the legal and financial implications in choosing a partnership type. Additionally, all parties involved in the business should consider signing a *legal partnership agreement* prior to engaging in business activities. This is important as it clearly defines roles and responsibilities for a partnership. More information regarding contracts will be provided later in this chapter.

There are three types of partnerships, and each of these will vary depending on your partnership needs and goals. These include:

- **General Partnerships**—In this partnership type, all profits, liability, and management duties are divided equally among the partners; there are options in this partnership for unequal distribution, but only if this is noted in the partnership agreement.
- **Limited Partnerships**—This is also referred to as a partnership with limited liability. This type of partnership is more complex than a general partnership.

It allows for some partners to have limited liability and even limited input in the business, depending on the terms of the agreement. This can be a useful partnership type if the business partners include investors only interested in short-term or limited-term projects.

- **Joint Ventures**—This type of partnership is distinguished as a partnership only for a single project or for a limited amount of time. Joint ventures can be used in ongoing or long-term projects, but only if the partners note this when filing paperwork.

Once a partnership type is determined, the partners will need to file the appropriate paperwork. The paperwork to register a business is determined by the state in which the business resides, and those forming a business should examine such documents found on their state department's Web site and/or offices. In addition to filing general business paperwork, the partnership must file for a legal business name. Partners should ensure in advance that no other businesses in the state have the same legal business name and that there are no copyright and/or trademark infringements. Should the partners choose to use a fictitious name (i.e., a name different from the legal business name) to conduct their business, then they will need to file an additional note that they are operating under an assumed name, trade name, or "doing business as" (DBA) name.

For partnerships, businesses are required to register with federal and state entities and obtain a federal business ID number, called a federal Employer Identification Number (EIN). Partnerships do require that the partners file additional information on their tax returns, as opposed to a sole proprietorship where the taxes are filed as an individual. In general, these include annual return of income, employment taxes, and excise taxes, reported on Form 1065. In addition, the partnerships are responsible for income tax, self-employment tax, and estimated tax, as applicable, and these taxes are filed under each partner's personal tax returns.

Quick Facts about Partnerships:

- **Liability**—In a general partnership, all partners assume responsibility for the partnership's debts and other obligations. A limited partnership has both general and limited partners, and in this case, the general partners assume liability for the partnership, whereas the limited partners serve as investors and do not assume any liability. Joint ventures function in much the same way as a general partnership, but are only for a specific amount of time or single project. Because of this, limited liability does not apply, as it does with limited partnerships; therefore, all partners in a joint venture are liable for any financial and/or legal obligations.

- **Paperwork**—State law controls the formation of a partnership business. The Secretary of State Web site for each state should provide business requirements unique to that state. In addition, the partnership will need to file for a federal EIN. Business names should be filed for at the state level, and if necessary, the partners should also file for trademark protection if they choose to legally protect the intellectual property of their legal business name.

- Taxes—A partnership requires filing an additional information return for tax purposes. Partnership income and expenses are reported on Form 1065. Any income or expenses reported should be filed by each partner on their personal tax return.

Corporation

A corporation (also known as a C corporation) is a legally separate entity with a complex business structure that requires it to comply with additional regulations. Corporations are owned by shareholders rather than individuals. Unlike some other business entity types that we have already examined, the shareholders who own the corporation are not liable for any legal issues and/or debt associated with the corporation, but rather, the liability resides with the corporation itself. This is important, as it helps protect the personal assets of the owners. Because there are so many complexities both legally and structurally, corporations are often formed by larger, more established businesses.

Like partnerships, paperwork to register a business as a corporation is determined by the state in which the business resides. Documents for filing for a business as a corporation are found on a state department's Web site and/or office. Additionally, corporations need to file a legal business name.

Corporations are required to register with federal and state entities and obtain a federal business ID number (the EIN). In addition, corporations need to make sure that they obtain the proper business licenses and permits—a distinction that sets this business entity type apart from the previous entities examined. Because regulations on licenses and permits vary by industry, state, and locally, businesses registering as corporations should make sure to do proper research on the appropriate paperwork prior to registering. There are additional considerations with regard to corporations with employees as well, and those considering a corporation will want to explore those items with a financial professional.

Taxes for corporations are more complex than those previously discussed for sole proprietorships and partnerships. Unlike those two business entities, corporations are required to pay income tax on any profits, and in some cases, the corporation will be taxed twice when earnings are distributed to shareholders in the form of dividends. These dividends are taxed at individual tax rates on personal tax returns. When filing taxes, corporations use Form 1120 or 1120-A.

Quick Facts about Corporations:

- **Liability**—The corporation is responsible for all of its own financial and legal liabilities, which protects the personal assets of the owners.
- **Paperwork**—Corporations are formed under the laws of each state. Once a business registers as a corporation, it is required to set up a formal structure consisting of shareholders, directors, and officers.
- **Taxes**—A corporation is required to file a separate income tax return: Form 1120. Any earnings distributed to shareholders in the form of dividends are taxed at individual tax rates on their personal tax returns.

Subchapter S Corporation

Because corporations are usually for larger, more established businesses, smaller businesses may not find a traditional corporation to be their best option. However, the subchapter S corporation, a variation of the standard corporation that we explored previously, may be an option that proves viable for smaller businesses—giving the business owners the benefits of a corporation without some of the complexities. Like standard corporations, the liability in S corporations is assumed by the corporation itself rather than the individuals. One distinct difference between S corporations and standard corporations is that the income or losses are "passed through" to individual tax returns, similar to a partnership.

Businesses need to adhere to certain shareholder limit thresholds in order to qualify to operate as an S corporation. This includes having no more than 100 shareholders in the corporation. Like standard corporations, S corporations are required to have directors and shareholder meetings and keep other legal documentation for any shareholder communications.

Paperwork for S corporations is virtually the same as a standard corporation, and like standard corporations, is subject to state law with regard to formation, including filing for a business, business name, and other paperwork-related matters.

As mentioned, taxes for S corporations function similarly to those in a partnership. Because income passes through to shareholders, regardless of whether or not there are actual distributions, double-taxation for the S corporation is virtually removed. S corporation shareholders file taxes using Form 1120S.

Quick Facts about S Corporations:

- **Liability**—S corporations are responsible for all of their debts and liabilities, which protects the personal assets of the owners.

- **Paperwork**—S corporations have the same corporate structure as a standard corporation and are formed under state laws.
- **Taxes**—S corporations file Form 1120S, U.S. Corporation Income Tax Return. Income passes through to shareholders whether or not there are actual distributions.

Limited Liability Company

Limited liability companies (LLC) offer those who choose it as a business entity the flexibility of a partnership with the limited liability benefits of a corporation. LLCs, like many of the business entities examined in this chapter, vary by state statute. Owners of LLCs are referred to as "members," and depending on the state, an LLC owner may include a single member (i.e., one owner) or multiple members, including individuals, corporations, or other LLCs.

Filing an LLC business will vary depending on the laws of the state in which the business is formed. There are some particular requirements for an LLC that may be different than other business entities. In particular, when considering a name for a business, the business owner must adhere to three rules. The first is that the business name must be different from any other existing LLC in the state in which it resides. Second, the business must use the term "LLC" or "Limited Company" in the name of the business. And finally, the business name must not include words that are restricted by the state in which the business resides. When you register your business, your business name is automatically filed simultaneously, which means that the business owner does not need to follow any additional filing processes. Also, LLCs need to file articles of organization, a document that officially legitimizes the LLC, and the business should take note to obtain any business licenses and permits as needed. And finally, in some states, LLCs are required to announce their business formation locally in various news outlets, such as a newspaper. Those considering an LLC should consult with the state in which they reside to see if this is a requirement for their business.

Taxes for limited liability corporations are done through the individual owners, as the federal government does not recognize an LLC as a business entity; however, some states do recognize LLCs as a business entity and may be subject to state tax. It is recommended that those considering an LLC consult with local tax agencies to confirm if they are subject to state tax. Unless state taxes apply, all taxation is passed onto the members of the LLC through their personal taxes. Some additional considerations for tax purposes apply for LLCs; tax reporting varies upon the LLC classification. The default tax classification for an LLC with at least two members is a partnership. Those filing as a partnership will use Form 1065 for tax returns. A single-member LLC is disregarded as separate from its owner for income tax purposes. In this case, a single-member LLC will file taxes using Form 1040, Schedule C, like a sole proprietorship. And finally, an LLC may also elect classification as a corporation for tax purposes only. In this case, the LLC will use Form 1120 for tax purposes. It is important to note that after an LLC has determined its federal tax classification, it can later elect to change that classification.

Keep in mind that one particular business structure is not necessarily better than any other. Ultimately, choosing a particular business structure will depend on an owner(s)' needs and business goals. Having a basic understanding of the different types can help you prepare to ask questions and think comprehensively when seeking advice from financial and legal experts.

Quick Facts about Limited Liability Corporations:

- **Liability**—Owners generally have limited personal liability for the debts and actions of the LLC but without the complexity of a corporation.

- **Paperwork**—LLCs are formed under the laws of each state. Once a business owner registers their business as a corporation, they are required to set up a formal structure according to state law.

- **Taxes**—Like a partnership, LLCs provide management flexibility and the benefit of pass-through taxation. Unlike other entity types, tax reporting depends upon the LLC classification. The default tax classification for an LLC with at least two members is classified as a partnership. A single member LLC is disregarded as separate from its owner for income tax purposes. An LLC may also elect classification as a corporation for tax purposes only. After an LLC has determined its federal tax classification, it can later elect to change that classification.

TAXES

Taxes may not be the most glamorous of details to consider when starting a consulting business; however, it is certainly one of the most critical financial pieces that you will need to handle, regardless of the business entity type that you choose as the foundation for your business. Reporting income, profit, and losses are all required per federal and state law, so it is important to understand important tax implications prior to filing taxes.

Like many other business considerations, taxes are dictated by the business structure that you choose. Reporting requirements vary, as indicated in the section earlier on business entities. It is advised that you consult with a professional tax preparer to determine if and what is required for you to file.

Regardless of business structure type, you need to have a basic recordkeeping system in place to keep track of income and any expenses to be reported. Having basic recordkeeping in place is not only a requirement in many cases, but is also good business practice to monitor the financial health of your business.

Developing a relationship with a tax professional can help ensure significant tax savings and planning strategies as your business grows. A tax professional can help you understand the tax implications of business decisions, including the costs of employees versus independent contractors, health care benefits, and retirement options. Such considerations should always be discussed with a legal and financial expert before implementing.

BOOKKEEPING AND ACCOUNTING

Bookkeeping and accounting essentials are necessary to keep track of your financial records and assess the health of your business. Bookkeeping includes the specific tasks of recording and categorizing your financial transactions, whereas accounting is the analysis and reporting of your financial records. Accounting tells the financial story of your business. It gives a snapshot of the current health of your business and provides insight to help you plan for future needs. Both go hand in hand and help you best keep track of your financial business records.

Bookkeeping specifically includes recording income, categorizing expenses, and reconciling bank accounts. It provides data to evaluate the financial health of your business and gives you, as a business owner, the ability to anticipate future needs and challenges. Following are some bookkeeping basics to help get you started. Additional links and resources can be found at the end of the chapter.

The primary goal for your bookkeeping system should be to streamline processes so that you are spending less time with bookkeeping and more time serving clients, which includes delegating and automating your bookkeeping processes.

Bank Accounts

One of the first steps that any business owner should take after selecting a business structure is to open a separate business account. Every business should consider opening the following accounts, separate from personal accounts, and regardless of business structure:

- **Checking Account**—This type of account should be utilized to track income and expenses.
- **Business Savings Account**—This type of account should be used for business owners to set aside a percentage of their income for self-employment taxes and for estimated income taxes.
- **Business Credit Card or Debit Card**—This type of account should be utilized only if the business owner plans on charging expenses. Most banks provide a debit card linked to the checking account, which can also serve as a "credit card" for tracking expenses.

Before you decide on specific accounts and even banking institutions, research the best financial accounts for your business needs. First, make sure to check with individual banks to compare their business account options, including fee structures. Financial institutions vary, and you will want to ensure you get the best financial scenario for your business needs. Of course, you can also do research at each financial institution's Web site for more information. It is important to note that most business checking accounts have fees that are higher than personal banking accounts, so pay close attention to the details, including required minimum balances and number of transactions.

Bookkeeping and Accounting Basics

The most basic bookkeeping system is simply recording your business income and expenses. More advanced bookkeeping includes categorizing transactions to capture the profits, losses, and tax deductions with continuous online bank reconciliations. Regardless of how simple or complex your bookkeeping needs are, having an effective bookkeeping system in place will allow you to measure your profits, minimize taxes, identify cost-cutting opportunities, and help plan for future business growth.

Because most information specialist consultants are passionate about working with libraries and librarians, not crunching numbers, outsourcing bookkeeping services can help optimize your accounting and increase overall profitability. Outsourcing includes the use of online bookkeeping software, as well as hiring professional accounting and bookkeeping services. Fortunately, bookkeeping software and outsourcing options are abundant and inexpensive. Regardless of which option you choose, outsourcing your bookkeeping from the beginning will ensure that you have a solid system in place that can be used to monitor the health of your business throughout the year and one that prepares you for tax season.

Today's online business environment offers outsourced bookkeeping at a reasonable price for business owners of all levels. Regardless of what bookkeeping avenue you choose, it is worth taking the time to fully explore your options and determine what might work best for you. Here are some possible sources for bookkeeping services:

- **Professional Bookkeeper**—Ensure that they are certified and experienced.
- **QuickBooks Online**—Includes tools such as apps and other integrations, timesheets, expense reporting, and job costing.
- **QuickBooks Self-Employed**—A straightforward tool for independent contractors. Key features include downloading bank transactions and allowing accountant access for ongoing monitoring and support.

When you are looking at of these resources and tools for bookkeeping services, think about these important considerations before selecting a particular service:

- Flexible—Does the service offer solutions that will allow it to grow with you and your business needs?
- Available—Is the service available in a variety of ways and during the times you need them? Do you have online access 24/7? Are there options for you to communicate in a variety of ways (e.g., online chat, video chat, etc.)?
- Comprehensive—Do they provide a comprehensive set of resources that include tax planning and preparation? Do they provide you with monthly reports and other frequent and updated information to help you prepare for tax requirements such as estimated payments and self-employment taxes?

Regardless of what type of bookkeeping tool or service you use, it is important to know that the cost associated with it is certainly a worthwhile investment. Most of these services are surprisingly inexpensive, making them an affordable option for any independent consultant to consider. Additionally, consider the time and effort it will take you to do your own bookkeeping; compare it with the cost of a bookkeeper, and you will likely discover that an expert can do your bookkeeping at a fraction of the time. Investing in effective bookkeeping will provide you with a solid foundation for a resilient, forward-thinking business.

CONCLUSION

Though legal and financial considerations may seem like tedious areas of consulting, they need not be with some good research and input from legal and financial experts. With a basic foundation in this chapter, information professional consultants should be equipped with the tools and resources to get them started and on their way to legal and financial success in their business endeavors.

RESOURCES

Bench Accounting—Example of a comprehensive online bookkeeping service—https://bench.co/
Business Structures Checklist—https://bench.co/syllabus/
Godin, Seth. *The Modern Business Plan*. http://sethgodin.typepad.com/seths_blog/2010/05/the-modern-business-plan.html
IRS Business Structure Guide—https://www.irs.gov/uac/choosing-a-business-structure https://www.irs.gov/businesses/small-businesses-self-employed/business-structures
QuickBooks—Multiple offerings for online bookkeeping—https://quickbooks.intuit.com/

BUSINESS STARTUP CHECKLIST

- ☐ Develop a business plan
- ☐ Research basic knowledge of entity types
- ☐ Get complementary legal and tax advice, not in isolation
- ☐ Decide on the entity type
- ☐ File required paperwork
- ☐ Open bank account(s)
- ☐ Establish bookkeeping system—software or service
- ☐ Quarterly meetings/consulting to prepare for tax season
- ☐ Always inform accountant of potential decisions or changes!

5

Company Culture

Jamie Hollier and Tynan Szvetecz,
Commerce Kitchen and Anneal, Inc.

WHAT IS CULTURE? (HINT: NOT A PING PONG TABLE OR A BEER FRIDGE)

Your vision, values, systems, best practices, norms, beliefs, etc., all combine to create your company culture. It isn't about stuff; it is about the people and the actions that define the why, what, how, and who of your company's operations and identity.

Company culture isn't a mandate.

A healthy culture is collaborative and inclusive; it is a shared belief system. It can't be mandated by one person; there has to be buy-in and adoption across the organization. Company culture is about the people: the way that people are treated and treat one another, the way they communicate, the way they live their values, and the vision they share together.

However, company culture isn't just for large companies; it is part of what you are as a company, whether you are a sole proprietor or a Fortune 100. The independent contractor or solo proprietor works with teams on a regular basis, whether with other consultants or contractors or the team that is created when working with the clients. Contractors are commonly pulled into existing teams and cultures when they sign on to a project. So understanding what your culture is and how it relates to other cultures is key.

The culture of how you work, how you relate to others, and your vision of where you want to go all exist well before you even start your company. Your culture starts with you, so it has it be in alignment with who you are, where you want to go, and how you want to get there.

How You Do One Thing Is How You Do Everything

One thing learned after years as consultants is something you should definitely keep in mind as you strike out as an entrepreneur: "How you do one thing is how you do everything." Who you are, the good and the bad, will shape everything. Your strengths and weaknesses are not something that most people can change in drastic ways, so it is often your best approach to understand them and plan for them in your organization.

THE REALIZATION MOMENT FOR US

As the new year began in early 2015, the company we've presided over for 12 years began a new experiment. Once every six weeks, the entire organization would divide up into random teams and sit around a table together for a couple hours. The general goal was to provide a safe space for team members to give constructive feedback to each other. Through this feedback, we could become a team that was better, strong, faster.

Honest feedback can be illusive in small consulting groups and large organizations alike, and it was our hope that this type of ritual would encourage more regular constructive feedback outside of the formalized structure we created.

The ritual itself was derived from a technique discussed in Patrick Lencioni's book *The Advantage*, and subsequently expanded upon by the *Harvard Business Review*. For more information, visit https://hbr.org/2015/02/use-your-staff-meeting-for-peer-to-peer-coaching or http://www.wiley.com/WileyCDA/WileyTitle/productCd-0470941529.html.

Each team member's experience of the ritual is divided into two categories: positive reinforcement and constructive feedback. In the positive reinforcement phase, one team member listens as all the others reflect on something they admire about his or her approach and working style for no more than 30 to 60 seconds each. In the constructive feedback phase that happens subsequently, the same team member listens as the others note areas where they can improve, again for no more than 30 to 60 seconds each.

This was our *Open 360* experiment, and it failed. *Open 360*s are nothing new. Many of the most popular books on organizational culture in the Amazon store highlight *Open 360*s as one of the most important things you can do to become a learning organization and promote a culture of open dialog within a group. The benefits of having team members comfortable with offering candid feedback to each other are many.

In the influential and wildly popular book, *The Advantage: Why Organizational Health Trumps Everything Else in Business*, by Patrick M. Lencioni, the author argues that:

> *Contrary to popular wisdom and behavior, conflict is not a bad thing for a team. In fact, the fear of conflict is almost always a sign of problems.*
>
> *Why would team members who don't engage in conflict start to resent one another? When people fail to be honest with one another about an issue they disagree on, their disagreement around that issue festers and ferments over time until it transforms into frustration around that person.* (Lencioni 2012)

As *Open 360s* carried on, there was one very distinct trend: the very quality that inspired a team member to be complimented for their contribution to the team was also the quality that caused a team member to offer constructive criticism.

From the example:

- Team members *loved* that Jamie spoke her mind with clients and would lay everything out bluntly without the possibility for misunderstanding, but at other times they wished she would take it easier on them.
- The team loved that Jen could always understand where her clients and the team were coming from and admired her ability to be a terrific reader of people and empathic communicator, but at other times wanted to hear more about what she was really feeling deep down about a person or an issue.

The narrative of *Open 360s* became keep doing what you're doing *AND* dial back what you're doing. This phenomenon is a very human one: that the qualities that give us our natural strengths tend to also be the ones that give us our perceived weaknesses. It became clear that continuing with *Open 360s* in this way would water down our team's strengths as we worked to curb perceived weaknesses.

The next step was to explore a different approach that *humanized* the goal of building a culture of open and candid conversation. What was learned is that how you do one thing is how you do everything. By artificially putting a process in place that would restrain the natural strengths of the team in order to shore up weak spots, it would become an overall weaker team. The brilliance of individual talents would be diluted in an effort to keep the peace. It would unwittingly set a path to becoming homogeneous.

By choosing instead to celebrate a team member's strengths and to acknowledge that these same strengths can cause us to struggle in certain situations, the focus instead was on becoming more tactical with who is deployed when and where. Once strengths were viewed as an arsenal, custom configurations could be deployed depending on the challenge that needed to be solved; the process of stepping into the full potential of our team began. The culture became defined by strengths, rather than by efforts to "fix" weaknesses.

Seeing Yourself

Having insight into how you do things will help you to intentionally build a company culture in a way that fits with your natural inclinations. It is almost impossible to create a company that has values that are not in alignment with who you are, as you will end up spending more time struggling with that misalignment than on the care and tending of your work and your company. If there is one thing you can't squander on as an entrepreneur, it is the time and energy that you need to put into your company in productive ways. But to build this alignment, you need clarity on who *you* are. It is human nature to see our strengths and weaknesses through biased eyes.

One of the best ways to gather information about your natural inclinations in how you do things is to talk to people who know you well and who you trust to be completely honest with you.

Ask them about your good and bad habits. Ask them what makes you great, what value you bring to everything you do. Ask them what you do that drives them crazy.

This won't be easy, and you definitely need to have a thick skin for some of this, but if you have an open mind to feedback, it is way better to learn these things from a friend when you are starting out than from a client or colleague when you are trying to hold it all together.

There are some great tools to bring more insight as well. These two are the most commonly used in our companies:

- **Strengthsfinder** is a set of self-assessment tools that helps to frame where your natural strengths fall and what the impacts and implications of your profile mean for you as a person and an entrepreneur.
- **The Highland Ability Battery** is another great tool for gaining clarity into your strengths. What sets this test apart from the rest is that it is not a self-assessment, like Strengthsfinder, but a battery of skill assessment tests.

LEADERSHIP STYLES (BOTH INTERNAL AND EXTERNAL)

In the spirit of *how you do one thing is how you do everything,* your culture is a direct extension and manifestation of your leadership style.

Interestingly, leadership has a great deal in common with parenting, and it is the conscientious leader who will drive a more successful business culture forward, just as conscientious parents will set their children up for success in the long run.

Drawing on the extensive analysis and psychological research coming out of Cornell, the Center for Christian Counseling & Relationship Development (CCCRD), and Psychology Today, which have focused on understanding the most successful environments for children, we can likewise extrapolate and view the leadership spectrum through the following four lenses:

- The Authoritative Leader
- The Neglectful Leader
- The Permissive Leader
- The Authoritarian Leader

As a leader, you will have a style that is driven primarily by one of these four approaches, and it's important to note that this will also be the style that pervades your culture. This will happen regardless of any stated mission, or regardless of how many value statements are spread and shared across the organization.

Your leadership style will be subconsciously picked up and propagated by your colleagues, employees, and clients, and it will be magnified in their behavior toward each other when you are not around.

It is critically important for you to understand which leadership style you currently fall into and work with professional coaches, colleagues, and available literature to evolve your style if you believe aspects of it are doing more harm than good.

The Authoritative Leader

Authoritative Leadership is the most effective and beneficial leadership style for growing a successful organization.

Authoritative Leaders are easy to recognize, as they are marked by the high expectations that they have of their staff and themselves and how they balance these expectations with providing robust support, personal coaching, and formal training for their people. These leaders are empathetic. They are team players. They are good listeners.

This type of leadership creates the healthiest culture for a staff (or projects) and helps to foster a productive relationship between founders, executives, and employees.

How to recognize if you are an Authoritative Leader:

- Your team knows what's expected of them.
- Those expectations are consistent from day to day.
- You collaborate with your team on defining and evolving expectations together as time moves on. As a team, you are always willing to adapt to

changes in the work environment and with clients and agree on how team members can shift their efforts to benefit the whole team.

- You set aside a regular, recurring time to connect with individual team members one on one.
- You do this in the neighborhood of monthly rather than yearly.
- You are fair with how you hold members of your team accountable, and in the event that a team member is not meeting expectations, you move quickly to help them be more successful at a different organization.
- You value transparency and let your team in on your thinking, offering an articulate lay of the land while also providing room for feedback and comments.

These traits mark a healthy work environment. One of the most important traits to emulate in the Authoritative Leadership style is open communication with your team.

As an independent consultant who follows the Authoritative Leader approach, you will be the sort of person who strikes a balance between listening and collaborating with your client yet being firm in the areas where you have expertise. This approach is often referred to as "gentle authority," and it is very helpful to remind yourself of this approach with clients. In order for this approach to be effective with clients, there needs to be an understanding that this is a collaborative relationship and you were brought in for your expertise, not to "do as you are told." The best clients have planned for your involvement; want to work with you; give you defined parameters for your project; and expect teamwork, leadership, and follow-through from you.

As an Authoritative Leader, if you can foster the ability to speak to your employees without judgment or reprimand, you will be more likely to have insight into the work experience of your staff and gain new understanding, which can help you deploy operational changes that will make the team and the organization stronger.

The Neglectful Leader

Unsurprisingly, the Neglectful Leader is one of the most harmful types of leaders. Neglectful Leadership is unlike the other styles in that leaders can easily fall into the trap of "tuning out" the day-to-day challenges and stresses of work, typically in response to being overwhelmed with responsibilities and the constant pressure put on leaders to have all the answers.

If you recognize yourself as a Neglectful Leader—even some of the time as a response to stress—or if a colleague recognizes that they may know a Neglectful Leader in your organization, it is important to understand that those leaders need assistance. Often these leaders are in a rut and are struggling with their relationship to their work and their staff. They need help getting back on track to having a healthy and communicative relationship within their team.

If you suspect you or a colleague may be a Neglectful Leader, look for the following traits:

- Delegating tasks and challenges to staff without understanding the environment in which they must be executed
- Not asking direct questions about the nature of a problem
- Waving off challenges team members or clients are having
- Lack of motivation to get going in the morning
- General lethargy
- Manifesting behaviors or symptoms that can overlap with those seen in clinical depression

If this describes you or someone you know, your business is at risk of having a dysfunctional culture and at risk of being railroaded by another team member who may not be the best individual to set the cultural tone of the organization.

Leaders who tend toward neglectful leadership styles can be helped through education and support. This can range from joining peer advisory groups such as Vistage, EO, or local chamber meetups, to engaging in counseling with a trained professional.

Neglectful Leadership can be very dangerous for sole proprietors. Leaving details to the very end, forgetting or missing elements, not communicating often and fully, etc., are all elements of neglectful leadership and create a negative experience for your clients.

Neglectful Leadership is damaging to any organization, because it creates apathy among the staff. It can also lead to operational problems simmering and festering, which could ultimately lead to a catastrophic failure to perform for clients or stakeholders.

The Permissive Leader

Permissive Leadership, also known as Indulgent Leadership, is another potentially harmful style of leading.

In this style, you are a leader who is responsive but not demanding. You tend to be lenient while trying to avoid confrontation. The benefit of this leadership style is that you embrace a nurturing and loving approach to your people and their work. At first, people can find you pleasant and easy to be around.

However, the negatives quickly mount over time and greatly outweigh any benefit. There is little in the way of accountability among the staff working under Permissive Leaders, and the enforcement of accountability is spotty and inconsistent when it does arise.

This lack of structure causes a sense of frustration among team members, because some will be working smarter or more efficiently and skillfully than others while seeing mistakes and poor performance essentially ignored. This breeds resentment over time and can lead to talented team members leaving the organization entirely.

Additionally, many team members will develop a sense of insecurity related to their performance. What is being expected of them? Are they performing well or not? All things being equal, most people want to contribute and do good work. If it's not clear what the standard is, your staff is being deprived of the rewarding feeling that comes from meeting the standards of performance in your organization.

As a sole proprietor you may find yourself doing things not originally in the contract or backing down on certain essential solutions because you want to avoid confrontation, you want to keep the client happy. You may make promises that you cannot keep. You "take sides" in a situation that is not conducive to your mission.

How to recognize if you are a Permissive Leader:

- Members of your team are making the same mistake repeatedly (making a mistake is one thing; making the same mistake over and over should not be happening in a functional organizational culture).
- There is a wide divergence in efficiency and speed between your top performers and your bottom performers.
- You trust only certain top performers in your team with mission-critical tasks.
- There are trust issues between members of your team.

Developments along these lines indicate an unhealthy permissive leadership style. On the surface, it may seem as though this would be an employee's favored way to be led as it provides a sense of freedom without consequences. However, many people tend to crave a sense of structure that ensures they understand the expectations of those around them. This frames their work so they can rise to meet those expectations.

Meeting expectations is an important mark of contribution and self-esteem for employees, and it has been proven to increase employee retention and loyalty.

If you are an independent Permissive Leader, you will often find yourself unable to provide the value you want to your clients. You will often give in to unrealistic demands, allow for decisions to be made that you don't believe in, and will often find yourself working really hard for very little reward (financially and emotionally).

On the other hand, permissive clients want you to make all the decisions, and it can be difficult to get information from them. This often means that the expertise or knowledge that they need to bring to your work is missing and makes it difficult for you to do a good job.

The Authoritarian Leader

If you are an Authoritarian Leader, you are characterized by being demanding but not responsive. Your communications with your team are often curt and critical and can border on aggressive or "mean."

Authoritarian Leaders allow for little open dialogue between themselves and employees or clients and expect them to follow a strict set of rules and expectations without question. They usually rely on public embarrassment and ridicule to enforce performance.

As a sole proprietor you are rigid and insist on your solution without paying attention to the unique situation. You come in, barrels blazing, to "save the day." This is never effective.

Here are some indications you may be falling into an Authoritarian Leadership style:

- You have very strict rules that you believe should be followed no matter what.
- You often find yourself offering no explanations for the rules other than "Because I said so."
- You give your employees little leeway to decide how they would solve a problem.
- You micro-manage your employees' activities in pursuit of resolving a task.
- You are reserved in the amount of warmth and nurturing you show your team.

While the structure an authoritarian leader imposes could be necessary for a healthy organization, if it feels didactic and arbitrary, it will drive your team to underperform.

It is important to balance out the provided structure with open communication so employees know exactly why it is important for them to meet the standards placed in front of them. An organization that follows an Authoritarian Leader will manifest the following qualities:

- Employees will not be inspired or motivated to suggest process changes that could lead to a better-performing team.
- Employees will spend more time in "CYA" mode than collaborating.
- There will be a lack of cheer or humor around the office.
- Employee turnover will be high.
- Customer loyalty will be below the standards of your industry.

Authoritarian Leadership styles for an individual consultant translate to not listening to the client's needs and pushing through personal agendas. Rather than understanding that all people in a project bring knowledge and expertise, this leadership style sees value only in their opinions and approaches. This philosophy will disempower your clients and can pretty much guarantee that they do not choose to work with you again in the future.

Working with a client who is an Authoritarian Leader is also dangerous. They usually have strict agendas and goals they want to see you achieve, whether it is the right approach for the organization or not. Often they hire you to "do the dirty work."

The People: Jazz as a Model

The people you work with, the unique mix of their personalities, skills, communication style, preferences, etc., will come together a little differently in any group. Each person is unique, and therefore each collection of people is also unique, and that combination will be a defining element to your culture.

One way to think about this mix is to compare it to improvisational jazz. Here are a few concepts from jazz that carry over into company culture:

1. Everyone needs to know the basics of their role, their part. When a collection of accomplished jazz musicians come together, there is a shared understanding pretty quickly, even if they have never played together before. This shared understanding comes from being able to see differences and similarities, nuances in style, through playing a piece of music that all know well.

2. This shared understanding and common language is core to a well-functioning team. In our organization, we use the concept of group norms to bring that shared understanding. Group norms are a collection of guiding principles, ideas, and approaches that everyone agrees to operate within. They can be as broad reaching as our core values or generosity of spirit, gentle authority, and ownership or as tactical and concrete as the list of the technology we use for our code deploys.

3. Listening is the most important part of cooperation and collaboration. The reason that jazz improvisation works is because everyone playing is spending most of their energy listening. In order to play well with a diverse group, you have to hear them fully and focus on that first above what you want to do and how you want to play. The focus is on listening and then complementing and collaborating.

4. This concept holds true in all our relationships, especially working ones. Everyone has to be equally open to listening to and bending a little to others' ideas and approaches. In technology, it is not uncommon to find people who have a great amount of skill and have historically been in positions where they were empowered to do their own thing, to become an independent rock star. It is consistently found that the individual with fewer skills but more interest in collaboration and commitment to listening first has always provided more value to the organization over "rock stars."

5. Flexibility in how you play is key to success. You will never have only the team you choose as a jazz musician or as an entrepreneur. You and your

team will always find yourself working with a diversity of other people, whether they are your clients, other contractors, vendors, or even stakeholders. Jazz musicians are used to showing up to a performance and being comfortable with a slightly fluid role—for one gig your approach and style may take the lead with others taking a more complementary role, and your next gig may require you to take a step back and have more of a supporting role, or as often happens, this may shift throughout the gig itself.

It is important for you and your team to be comfortable with shifting gears across and within your different projects. Small companies especially must be open to adding value where and how they can without feeling uncomfortable with allowing others to take center stage or being asked to step up to center stage yourself.

THE ROLES

There are a few relationships that are specific and important enough that we want to highlight our own perspective and a few thoughts about each of these roles.

Individual Owner or Partnership

There are benefits to both sides of either going it alone or building a team when you start your entrepreneurship journey, or even as you progress down that path.

As an individual you create your own culture and choose who you will work with and when. Of course, this doesn't mean you are alone. You become a de facto team member with every contract.

In a partnership the burdens are often easier to bear when you can share them with another person; even if that only means you have someone to commiserate. The ideas and approaches are more robust and creative when you have more than one person working through problems and solutions. Lastly, you are able to staff your weaknesses when you have more than one person involved, as none of us can do it all and be good at everything.

However, owning a business with someone is a serious commitment. In many ways, you will spend more time and share more challenges with the person you own your company with than you will with your spouse or significant other. And you run the same risks. Owning a business means you have to have shared vision, shared goals, the same driving forces, similar risk tolerance, etc., or conflict will quickly arise. If you think you want to share a company with another person, be very thoughtful about where you have shared understanding and where you differ, as those will be the make-or-break elements of your partnership. Additionally, be prepared for things to change and for this relationship to fail from the beginning. It may sound pessimistic, but just like a marriage, no one intends to get divorced, but life is unpredictable, so plan both personally and professionally (with your legal documents, etc.) for the potential of a breakup. For more on formal partnerships see Denise Shockley's Chapter 4.

Hiring (Fit over Skills, Trust, etc.)

You can be the best leader in your industry, write the greatest employee handbook, and have the coolest office in town, but it will all be for naught if you don't find and hire the right people.

AN EXAMPLE

Two years ago, we decided to change our hiring and interviewing process entirely to reflect our culture. We constantly ask for our employees' feedback and opinions on current strategies, clients, projects, and so on. The logical way to approach hiring was to treat it like anything else we do. Thus, team interviews were born.

Once a potential hire, their resume, and references have been vetted, we bring in that person for a series of two interviews that last a total of two hours. The first hour is a resume review and leadership team interview. The leadership team and whoever else wants to join sit down with the person and talk about their history. The second hour is when we bring in the rest of the team—developers, QA, sales, all of them—into the room, and the leadership team leaves. The team interview gives the person a chance to hear about working at Commerce Kitchen without leadership in the room, and it gives our employees a chance to ask the potential hire more technical questions.

This interviewing strategy really changed the game for us. We found that candidates who the team was uncertain or wary about were probably not the right fit, and the ones who the team liked the most ended up being great fits. It's when we have strayed from this format—i.e., not properly vetting and interviewing a candidate—that it's come back to bite us in the end.

When you hire a person for their fit—the potential growth of skills, culture fit with the team, etc.—they are more likely to be a successful team member than those whom we've hired based on skill alone.

Even independent consultants will need to understand hiring and firing techniques for work with fellow consultants, hiring contractors or subcontractors, and even when you are meeting with prospective clients. It is not uncommon for your working relationship with your clients and contractors to be a defining factor in your success, so don't be shy about turning down or even firing clients and contracts that prove to be a bad fit culturally. See Melissa Stockton's Chapter 7 for more on "When to Say No."

Vendors and Partners

Those that provide services to your company can have just as much impact as those within it on your culture and success. Find vendors (lawyers, accountants, etc.) and subcontractors that share your approach to business, your level of professionalism, and your commitment to your values. Risk tolerance is a big one here.

For example: In some industries with a high level of risk (such as HIPAA compliance), you may prioritize having a lawyer with a lot of experience who knows you, knows your approach, and knows how to protect you and minimize your risk. A lawyer who shares your values, who puts compromise above conflict and walks that line for you perfectly. This choice is by no means a cheap one, but that prioritization of this role could be imperative to your company's well-being.

The same can be said for subcontractors. Be wary of working with untested vendors and spend the time and energy to fully vet them. It will save you from paying for it financially and emotionally. Anyone who will be doing work that reflects on you and your company needs to be considered as strongly as you would your own staff. At the end of the day, their work and their approach become a part of the product or service you provide.

WHERE YOU ARE CAN AFFECT HOW YOU ARE

One of the most important decisions you can make when you are setting out on your own is where you work. The good news is that there are a lot of different options and enough flexibility with many of them for you to experiment with different spaces fairly easily. Each person has their own approach and style for what works best for them, and it may take some time to figure out what works best for you and when, as different types of spaces can be conducive to different types of work.

Home Offices

Home offices are where most people start out, and the benefits are pretty clear. One of the main benefits of a home office is that it provides you with flexibility around when, where, and how you want to work, which can be incredibly valuable while you are still starting off and are figuring out what times and ways you prefer to work. Additionally, working from home can save you a lot of money, not only because you don't have to pay for an office space but also because you are not spending money on commuting, parking, and eating out. Those coffees on the way in can add up pretty quickly!

However, home offices are not for everyone and have their definite downsides. Although you may be saving time without a commute, you may also find yourself getting distracted by the laundry or the other chores at home. Trying to create separation between your personal life and your professional one is harder the other way around as well. Not only do you find yourself doing dishes when you should be working, you will likely find yourself drawn to your computer when you should be spending time with family. In addition to this, most people find it harder to emotionally disconnect from work and are quicker to burn out with a home office.

Isolation can be a wonderful part of working from home, or it can be a great hindrance to your productivity. You may find that the type of work you are doing is the driving factor for when you work alone or with others. For example, if you have to think through a difficult user flow to get a first draft of it together, you may want to do that at home where you have more ability to limit interruptions and really focus. However, once that user flow is hashed out, you may find that you want to work with others on that piece as thinking out loud and being questioned about elements of your process undoubtedly improve the final product. Regardless of whether you can directly work with others or not, sometimes just having social interactions with others and being in a livelier environment can help you think differently. Thinking about how much time you like to spend with others and what kind of work you will mostly be doing will help you decide how to balance a home office.

One of the other major factors in deciding if a home office is right for you is thinking about whom your clients are and how you will engage with them. If you will be meeting with clients in person, often having an appropriately professional and furnished space for these meetings is important.

If you are thinking the home office is the right fit for you at the moment, here are a few tips to make it work best for you:

1. Have a dedicated space. Having a desk with all the tools, supplies, and personal touches to make it feel like your "office" can go a long way. Try to create a space that is separated from the distractions of daily life, if possible, such as in a guest room away from the dishes and a place that signals to your family that when you are there, you are working.

2. Create rituals around "going" to work. It is easier to prevent burnout and to be more productive if you try to create more separation between your work and personal lives. Set schedules for your work time and try to stick to those. Get dressed in the morning. It doesn't have to be fancy like you were going to a traditional office but staying in your pajamas all day, although it sounds great, usually doesn't help you feel accomplished.

3. Think about how you like to work, and plan your days around your style and the types of work you will be doing. If you are a more extroverted

person who needs more social engagement, maybe you should plan to work at a coffee shop or in a co-working space for a little bit each day or for a couple of days a week. We will discuss more about these options in the next sections.

Coffee Shops

If you want to go with a home office, you should also find some coffee shops in your area (or similar places) that are friendly to remote workers. This is a good option for people who like the hustle and bustle of a coffee shop environment. Similar to a home office, the best time and place to go to a coffee shop or similar location depend on your style and preferences for working.

While coffee shops can provide the interactions and activity you may crave in your work at times, they are far from the perfect place to work full time. One major issue is the cost. Not every coffee shop is open to people coming in and buying one cup of coffee before camping out for hours. Even if you are lucky enough to find a spot welcoming to remote workers, you still need to buy something every time you go, and that can add up quickly for someone trying to start a new business. In addition, having to set up a new working space each time can be a time sink, depending on the shop; you may need to pack up your stuff each time you go to the bathroom in order to ensure your belonging are secure. Add to that the difficulty of finding a spot to work, an outlet to plug into, etc., and sometimes you spend more time trying to work than actually working when you go to a coffee shop.

If you would like to work from a coffee shop, here are a few ways to improve your experience:

1. Find the right shop. There are many shops out there that are very friendly to remote workers spending large amounts of time there, but many are not. Additionally, many shops are tiny, and people are always juggling for space but others are more spacious and will have plenty of room for you to set up. Finding a place where you don't have to worry about how long you have been there or how much space you are taking up makes the experience a ton more productive and engaging.

2. Bring your own Internet. Public Wi-Fi is not secure, so it is best to tether to your phone or bring your own hotspot to ensure that your data and your client's information are kept private. This is particularly important if you are working on anything that has a confidential nature to it.

3. Don't rely on coffee shops alone. They can be a great place to get exposed to a livelier atmosphere and can even spur more creativity, but they can be overwhelming if they are your only source for work space. They are best leveraged in combination with a home office or other, more private, workspace.

Co-Working Space

Co-working spaces are all the rage right now. For the most part that makes a lot of sense as they are a great next step up from the home office/coffee shop shuffle. While there is a significant financial cost to co-working when compared to home offices and coffee shops, there are a lot of benefits that make it well worth the investment.

One of the best things about a co-working space is that even if you are an individual entrepreneur, you can quickly become part of a like-minded community when you find the right co-working space. This sense of community can provide you with a network of subcontractors to fill any gaps in your services. Additionally, it can give you access to not just a more social environment, but the potential for more quality social interactions than you would get in a coffee shop by exposing you to a more regular group of people who are often in similar situations to yours.

In addition to the networking and social benefits of co-working spaces, the professional appearance and atmosphere are seen as an improvement over the home office for most. Many spaces are very well appointed with great meeting rooms where you can host clients, access to fast and reliable Wi-Fi, printers and copiers, and in some places front desk staff. Additionally, many people find the idea of getting dressed and heading out to work provides a routine that benefits their productivity and their work–life balance.

However, co-working can be less than ideal if you find a space that doesn't align well with who you are and how you want to work.

AN EXAMPLE

One of the co-working spaces my colleague and I tried out for a while felt a little too focused on being about hip new startups that were looking to exit as soon as they could make some money. For us, many of our colleagues in this space didn't connect with our goal of making a company we wanted to work while nurturing for the long term. Additionally, we were focused on working on projects that were important to us rather than ones that prioritized valuations and profits. As you can imagine, the culture of the space we were in and the culture we wanted for ourselves were out of alignment, and we moved within a few months.

Where you are really can contribute to shaping who you are, so be careful to ensure that the community you are thinking of joining is representative of your culture.

What kind of projects are you working on? Are they conducive to an open office/co-working space? You may end up working on projects with vendors who insist on confidentiality. Making sure your office space is properly secure is very important in these situations.

If you think co-working may be a good fit for you, here are a few thoughts on how to find a place where you will be happy and productive for the long run:

1. Test the waters with a few different options. Many co-working spaces offer day passes or other ways to try them out without any commitment. There are enough options in many locations that it is worth spending some time in a few of the different spaces to get a better feel for the atmosphere and culture and see which is in the best alignment for you. You will want to pay attention to the types of companies in the space, the friendliness of the staff, etc.

2. Sweat the small stuff. When you are shopping for a new office space, the little things can make a big difference in your day-to-day life. Notice if they provide free coffee and, if they do, how often do they run out or do they stay on top of keeping some freshly brewed? How hard is it to book one of the shared meeting spaces and how far in advance do you need to make your bookings? Is the space noisy, too hot, too cold, empty, bustling, etc? Are there enough plates and glasses in the kitchen, and does the heating system work well? These things can have major impacts on your productivity so pay attention to all the details in the space.

3. Decide what kind of space would be best for you. Many co-working spaces offer everything from a membership that gives you limited access to resources like the meeting rooms and no dedicated work space (you use the communal desks) all the way through to unlimited resources and your own private office within the space. Learn about all the options and decide what makes the most sense for your needs and your budget.

Your Own Office Space

If you are just starting out, it is unlikely that getting your own office space through a lease or purchase makes the most sense, but it can be an important step once you are more established as it provides more control over your company culture and direction. However, this is not a step to be taken lightly as it usually involves a significant and long-term financial investment.

Leasing, while less of a commitment than buying, is still a major step, as commercial leases are generally five years in length and often require personal guarantees from the business owners in more metropolitan areas. If you are sure you want your own dedicated office, it is often best to start out looking for a sublease or an executive suite, an individual or set of individual offices sublet from a larger suite of offices, as they can have shorter terms and more straightforward agreements.

If you decide to lease your own space, be sure to get your lawyer to review your commercial lease, as the lease types are very different from residential leases, and you will often find that you are responsible for paying additional fees such as the maintenance and repairs or the space and the taxes on the property. Additionally, many commercial leases require a personal guarantee from the company owners, meaning that if for some reason the company can't pay the rent you are personally on the hook for it.

Buying is often an important step for many companies as owning your building is a great way to gain the collateral that banks seek when considering whether to provide the necessary capital for company growth. However, the original capital for a purchase of this type can be a barrier and also increases your workload as you now have building maintenance on your plate in addition to the increased risk of decades of payments for which you are responsible.

If you get to the point where you are considering your own office space, whether leasing or buying, I strongly suggest that you get professional help from a commercial broker and a real estate lawyer to take these steps with the least risk.

CONCLUSION

There are many studies from the medical field that point to the idea that the doctors who get sued the least are the ones who have the best culture with their patients (Carroll 2015). The same is true for your company and how you work with others. Having a culture that fosters communication, engagement, and transparency is often more important to your success than the actual quality of work that you provide. People want to work with consultants that they believe they can trust, and trust comes from culture.

Culture is one of the main aspects that will define not only your external success in your endeavor, but also defines your own satisfaction, stamina, and commitment. Who you work with, whether clients, staff, subcontractors, or vendors, will define a great deal of how you spend your day. Add on top of that how a physical space aligns with your operational and emotional needs as an entrepreneur. The people you spend your time with and the places where you spend it will be the main defining aspects of the emotional impact that your work as an entrepreneur makes on your life. Do the work to find what fits for you, and you will find yourself doing better work and enjoying it more.

RESOURCES

Carroll, Aaron E. "To Be Sued Less, Doctors Should Consider Talking to Patients More," *The New York Times*, June 1, 2015. https://www.nytimes.com/2015/06/02/upshot/to-be-sued-less-doctors-should-talk-to-patients-more.html?_r=1
Highland Ability Battery. https://www.highlandsco.com
Lencioni, Patrick M. (2012-03-14). *The Advantage, Enhanced Edition: Why Organizational Health Trumps Everything Else in Business* (J-B Lencioni Series). Wiley. Kindle Edition.
Strengthsfinder. http://strengths.gallup.com/default.aspx

FURTHER READING

Logan, Dave. *Tribal Leadership: Leveraging Natural Groups to Build a Thriving Organization*. HarperBusiness, 2011.

Sinek, Simon. *Leaders Eat Last: Why Some Teams Pull Together and Others Don't*. Portfolio, 2014.

Walsh, Bill. *The Score Takes Care of Itself: My Philosophy of Leadership*, Portfolio, 2010.

6

Marketing and Branding

Crystal Schimpf, Kixal, Inc.

Marketing: the process or technique of promoting, selling, and distributing a product or service. (Merriam-Webster, Inc., 2014, 760)

As an independent consultant, you will need to market your services to potential clients. Without any marketing, libraries and other potential clients will not know what services you have to offer or why they should hire you. Marketing includes all of the branding, communications, publicity, advertising, and social media activities that you might engage in to promote your consulting business, develop relationships with potential clients, and ultimately sell your services. Marketing is an ongoing process made up of many different activities, not a single event, tool, or strategy (Levinson & Levinson, 2011, ch. 1).

In order to successfully market your library consulting or freelancing business, you should develop a marketing plan. This plan will help you identify goals for engaging in marketing activities, determine effective strategies for building business relationships, and set a budget for marketing and promotion. A marketing plan will also be a guide for you in practice and will give you something to measure the success of your efforts. A marketing plan is not a guarantee of success; however, it is a useful tool and can help you maximize your efforts.

This chapter will focus primarily on branding and communication, with an emphasis on networking, e-mail, and social media channels. These areas tend to have the lowest cost (Levinson & Levinson, 2011, ch. 2) and the greatest return for independent consultants, particularly in the library industry.

DEFINING YOUR BRAND

A brand is not a logo or a name. A brand is the complete identity you give to your consulting or freelancing business. As a consultant or freelance, your name (and your business name, if you have one) will be one of the most prominent identifiers of your brand. Your logo, if you choose to have one, will also be a primary identifier. However, other aspects of your brand, although not as visible, are critical to the success of your business as a consultant or freelancer.

Your brand includes the mission, purpose, and values that drive you to do your work. Your brand is a persona and includes your personality, social style, and work style. As an individual providing a service, your brand can include your personal interests, hobbies, and passions (or at least those that you choose to make public). Your brand extends to every piece of printed material, every social media post, all of your online accounts, and your appearance. Your brand is evident in every piece of work you create, every message you communicate, and in your personal associations and professional affiliations.

Having a consistent brand will help potential clients and customers understand who you are, the work you do, and why they should hire you. The value of the brand lies in its ability to sell your services to potential clients. Seth Godin, internationally recognized entrepreneur and writer, has this to say about the purpose of having a brand:

> A brand is the set of expectations, memories, stories and relationships that, taken together, account for a consumer's decision to choose one product or service over another. If the consumer (whether it's a business, a buyer, a voter or a donor) doesn't pay a premium, make a selection or spread the word, then no brand value exists for that consumer. (Godin, 2009)

How do you begin to define your personal brand? Previous chapters have taken you through many of these concepts. Now is the time to look inward and reflect on why you have chosen to become a library consultant or freelancer and answer these questions:

- How would you describe your business in one sentence?
- Who is your customer or client?
- What is your goal for having a business?
- Why have you chosen to do this type of work?
- What makes you special in the industry?
- What sets you apart from competitors?
- What is your mission or statement purpose for your business?
- What values inform your decisions in work and in life?
- What personal interests define you as a person in work and in life?

Take time to really think about these questions and reflect on what you are bringing to your business as a consultant. Write down your responses and save them for future reference. The way you define your brand will influence your decisions as you develop marketing materials.

DESIGNING A LOGO

A logo is a visual marker for your consulting or freelancing business. A logo can be used in business cards, print materials, social media profiles, images, and videos. A logo is not a monogram or a stylized version of your business name, although many people use these in place of logos. A logo is a visual representation of your brand and will include graphic and text elements.

A logo should be created by a competent graphic designer. A logo is something you shouldn't change often, so consider the cost an investment in your business. There are many online services for logo design, all with varying costs and varying value. Be wary of low-cost services that promise to deliver a logo for less than $100—you may get something that you can call a logo, but it may not have any representation of you, the work you do, or your brand identity.

There are many freelance graphic designers with reasonable rates, and you may want to ask around for referrals and recommendations. When you choose a graphic designer, ask them about their logo design process. Try to find a graphic designer who wants to learn about the work you do, your customers, and the values that drive your work. Remember, your logo should be a graphic representation of your brand.

When you work with a graphic designer, you can also ask for other brand elements and collateral, such as:

- Business cards
- Typeface, color palette, and style guidelines for print materials
- Other versions of the logo for use in social media
- Slide template for presentations
- Document templates such as letterhead, handouts, or bookmarks
- Stickers or other promotional items

CREATING A WEB SITE

A Web site is an important part of your image as a consultant or freelancer. It is the Internet location where you have the most control over how to display and share information about the work that you do. A Web site does not have to be complicated or expensive, but it should be given careful thought and updated regularly.

Your Web site should contain several key components. There are also several components you may want to include, depending on the nature of your work (see Table 6.1).

TABLE 6.1. Key Components to Include in Your Web Site

About your business	Provide a brief description of the work you do, the experience you've had, and the reasons you have for choosing this area of work. This is the biography of your brand. You may opt to include personal details or a personal biography, but remember that this Web site is representing your brand. You don't have to include everything.
Statement of purpose	This is an opportunity for you to reference your ethics and values as a consultant. What is it that drives you to work for libraries? If you work for clients outside of libraries, how do libraries fit into the bigger picture?
Services you provide	This may be a list of the types of services you provide, workshops you deliver, or packaged services. Include descriptions of the services to help people gain a better understanding of the nature of your work.
Examples of past and current work	This can be a list of clients, projects, presentations, events, or partners. It is best to include samples when possible. Always ask clients if it is okay to showcase samples on your Web site, especially when the work completed is proprietary or intended for internal use only.
Testimonials	Ask former clients to share a few words about the value of your services.
Contact information	What is your preferred method of contact? How can new business leads reach you? If you use a specific e-mail account or phone number just for this purpose, be sure to check it regularly or have the messages forwarded.
Blog (optional)	If you plan to write regularly, you may want to include a blog on your Web site. A blog is a place where you can post updates, share new ideas, and showcase the work that you do. However, if you don't think you will have time to blog, you may want to consider other sources for sharing. A blog should be updated regularly or else it will appear stagnant and outdated.
Calendar (optional)	If you regularly give workshops, webinars, or keynote addresses, you should include a calendar of your public appearances. This will let people know where to find you and how they can register to attend.
Rates (optional)	Some consultants and freelancers publish their rates. Others do not. Publishing your rates is one way to set a bar and let potential customers know what to expect. If you do wish to publish your rates, you can include it with the services you provide or include it as a separate page. If you do not wish to publish your rates, you will want to include some invitation to ask for a quote on your services or contact page.
Social media links and feed (optional)	If you are actively using social media, you will want to include links to your social media accounts on your Web site. You can also include feeds from your social media that will auto-populate as you create new tweets and posts.

You need to decide if you want to design and build your own Web site or if you want to work with a Web designer. Many low-cost tools are available to help you build your own Web site with minimal coding skills. If you are just getting started and have a limited budget, you may want to start with a "do-it-yourself" option. If you have more experience with Web design and content editing, you may be comfortable building your own Web site. However, if you don't feel confident assuming the technological responsibilities of building and maintaining your site, it may be worth the expense to hire a Web designer to do the initial build and ongoing maintenance of your site. Keep in mind that maintenance will also include things like Web hosting, domain renewal, and security updates. If you are comfortable building your site but would like more support and assistance with maintenance, consider looking for a hosting company that offers additional services for a higher rate.

If you opt to create your own Web site, many tools can help. Here are some resources and tools to help you get started:

- Designing and Building
  - Wordpress (open source) https://wordpress.com/
  - Drupal (open source) https://www.drupal.org/
  - Wix (freemium) http://www.wix.com/
  - Squarespace (fee) https://www.squarespace.com/
- Hosting (Wilson, 2017)
  - A2 Hosting (fee) https://www.a2hosting.com/
  - WP Engine (fee) https://wpengine.com/
  - Host Gator (fee) http://www.hostgator.com/
  - Bluehost (fee) https://www.bluehost.com/
- Web design training and instruction
  - Katrinah.com (free, also on YouTube) https://katrinah.com/
  - Udemy (fee/free) https://www.udemy.com/courses/design/web-design/
  - Lynda.com (fee) https://www.lynda.com/

If you choose to work with a Web designer, they will likely walk you through a process to help determine what is best for you. Here are a few things you will want to keep in mind as you find, contract, and work with a Web designer:

- Finding the right person or company: There are many freelance web designers with reasonable rates. There are also companies that specialize in working with small businesses. Ask around for referrals and recommendations from colleagues. Your Web designer does not need to be physically located in the same place as you—all of the work can be done virtually. However, you will want to find someone who is sensitive to your needs and considerations and who is interested in learning more about the work you do and the clients/

customers you serve. You will also want to work with someone who understands that your Web site is an online extension of your brand and is willing to work with you to build a Web site that is representative of your brand identity.

- Guiding content and design: Find and share examples of Web sites you like with your designer. These examples will help give your designer an idea of what elements you would like to include. Also think about what content you would like to include in the site. Your Web designer will likely conduct an interview to help guide the development of your site and will have recommendations for the best ways to organize and arrange content. However, it is your responsibility to provide the content to the Web designer.

- Ongoing maintenance: A Web site requires ongoing maintenance and updating. This applies to the back end of the site as well as the content. On the back end, you will need to update the code periodically to improve security and functionality. On the front end, you should review and update content regularly to make sure it is accurately reflecting your current services and brand identity.

- Cost considerations: The cost of a Web site may seem like a lot, depending on your budget and the cost of the Web designer you choose. But compare that to the cost of your time if you were to design the Web site yourself. Also consider the value of engaging a competent Web designer and the quality of the final project. Ongoing costs include the time it takes to manage back-end maintenance, security and software updates, and domain renewal. It is possible to find companies that can help with all or some of the maintenance, which may be less expensive than the time and cost it will take to do it yourself.

There are some great examples of library consultant/freelance Web pages (and also some great examples from outside of libraries). Before you begin designing your own page, take a look around. Collect examples of pages you like, and notice what it is you like about them. You don't have to reinvent the wheel when it comes to your Web page. Draw inspiration from those who have been successful. Here are a few recommendations to get you started:

Carson Block: http://www.carsonblock.com/
In Figure 6.1, Carson Block's Web site is an example of one that clearly describes both his purpose and the services he provides as a consultant.

Emily Clasper: http://www.eclasper.com/
In Figure 6.2, Emily Clasper's Web site is an example of how to list out specific services, and it aligns with her personal branding.

Jason Griffey: http://jasongriffey.net/
In Figure 6.3, Jason Griffey's Web site shows an example of how to integrate blogging and other professional writing.

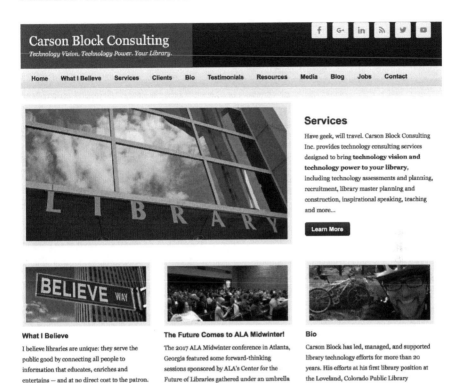

FIGURE 6.1. Carson Block Consulting

Patrick Sweeney: https://pcsweeney.com/
In Figure 6.4, Patrick Sweeney's Web site shows an example of how to include examples of your work to provide context for your services offered.

In addition to your own Web site, you may want to consider listing yourself in other library consultant Web sites or joining associations established for consultants. There may be a fee involved in this, but it is a way to increase exposure on the Internet. Here are a few examples of Web sites where you can list yourself as a consultant, freelancer, or speaker:

Association of Independent Information Professionals: http://www.aiip.org/
Library Consultants.org: http://libraryconsultants.org/
Library Consultants Interest Group (Association for Specialized and Cooperative Library Agencies): http://www.ala.org/ascla/interestgroups/iglc

FIGURE 6.2. Emily Clasper, Consulting

FIGURE 6.3. Jason Griffey, Blogging

As a library subject-specialist, I can speak on a variety of topics for your library school, association and library system. I am currently the Political Director for EveryLibrary and lecturer for San Jose State University iSchool, where I teach librarians about political activism. I offer full or half day staff training on political literacy skills, speaking and keynotes for staff development days, in-services, conference programs, and pre-conference workshops. As a library administrator I have the ability to relate to the workplace challenges and professional development goals of library staff, trustees, and friends. If you are looking for fresh and engaging presentation topics and styles, I have been providing these skills to libraries for the last nine years.

I have been a frequent speaker, presenter, and workshop leader at staff training days and library conferences around the country as well as a participant in the Great Library Roadshow. I was a 2015 Library Journal Mover and Shaker and my conference presentations are focused on supporting your conference theme with stories and best practices backed by data and research that are inspirational, motivating, and actionable for your attendees. I address individual outcomes as well as organizational engagement with relevant content to address your unique library community. Slides from a limited number of presentations are available on slideshare.

I am available for keynotes, breakout sessions, and half or full day workshops and trainings on a wide range of topics. I will work with you to develop the content for the session that

ORDER OUR BOOK!

Filled with easy to follow strategies, this book will guide ballot committees, librarians, trustees, and library advocates through the process of winning an election for funding their library.

FIGURE 6.4. PC Sweeney, Speaking At Your Event

CARSON BLOCK ON DESIGNING HIS OWN WEB SITE

How did you decide what information to include in your Web site and how to organize it?

"From the beginning, I envisioned my site as a place to collect relevant resources—so of course, information about me and my services, but also links to presentations, videos, materials, etc. I wanted the site to be simple—not flashy—with an emphasis on solid content instead of fancy and/or "hip" or trendy design. I want potential clients to know that although tech is my specialty, I'm also accessible to people of all levels of tech experience/comfort. I wanted it to be simple to scale (in both adding things and consolidating things) as new needs occurred over time. For instance, I added the "jobs" link when I began offering recruiting services for technology leader positions. Finally, I needed something that would be bone-simple to keep updated. My "office" (physical and virtual) is small (me plus a part-time assistant) so the structure needed to support easy updates."

Your personality really comes through in your site. What were some of your considerations in including these elements?

"With most consulting, the consultant and the client form a relationship in the process of addressing the work, so I think it's important that clients have a chance to know more about me before pursuing that relationship—not just what I can do for them in terms of results, but the way and manner that I go about it. I tend to work hard, and work with others who work equally hard or harder—and most of us spend the majority of our time working—so I try to find the fun, even in the midst of stressful situations. I think my orientation helps us do a better job together. I'm working with a partner who remarked to me yesterday—after facing a very stressful situation with a client and their vendor—'I'm glad you're on this project. You have a way of calming everyone down and helping us focus on solving the problems.'"

MARKETING WITH E-MAIL

One tool that is used by many independent consultants, freelancers, and small businesses is e-mail marketing. It has replaced direct mail as the primary way to send news and offers to potential customers and clients. E-mail is a low-cost method of communication (and can even be free, depending on the size of your audience and the e-mail marketing tool you use). However, just because everyone else is doing it and it doesn't cost much, doesn't mean it is the right choice for your business. Just like any other marketing choices you make, you need to think about how it might benefit your business and any hidden costs that you may not be considering.

There are many benefits to e-mail marketing. You can reach a large group of people with a single message. You can track the effectiveness of your e-mail campaigns using the analytic features of your e-mail marketing tool. E-mail messages can be easily forwarded, making it possible for you to reach an even wider, unknown audience (Sernovitz, 2012, p. 131). E-mail marketing can be used to drive traffic to your Web site or to increase new business during slow periods. E-mail can help build credibility in your areas of expertise and promote the specific services you offer. It can also be used to build and strengthen relationships with current and future clients (Pinkham, 2015).

There are also some hidden costs and common challenges to e-mail marketing. Hidden costs include the time it takes to create content, design e-mail templates, input content, create mailing lists, and track success of individual campaigns. One of the most common challenges to creating effective e-mail marketing is creating a message that people will want to open and read, especially when there are so many other e-mails sent and received on a daily basis. Over time you will want to test different subject headings and content styles. Another challenge is to consider the various devices that your e-mail might be viewed on and test out your template for readability. Many e-mail marketing platforms allow you to preview what your message will look like on a mobile device. You want to be sure your most important (or catchiest) content appears at the top. Include a call to action in your e-mail, whether it is to visit your Web site, send an e-mail, or dial a number; a call to action can help you determine if your effort was indeed effective.

If you are considering e-mail marketing, you will want to review what tools and platforms are available for you to use. There are many to choose from, such as MailChimp and Constant Contact. You should never send e-mail marketing direct from your e-mail account, though. Not only are there technical and privacy issues with sending a blanket e-mail to a large group of people, but you will not be able to track the success of your campaigns. Try to choose an e-mail marketing platform that has a good user interface. You may need to spend some time learning your way around, but if the interface feels clunky or confusing, it may not be the right tool for you. You should also compare cost and features. Are analytics only available at higher price points? Is there a limit to the number of people you can e-mail in a single day? Does the platform provide any support at the free or lower-tier cost levels?

Once you decide on an e-mail marketing platform, you can take the time to build your templates and content strategy. How frequently will you send out an e-mail? Will you pull content from your blog or from social media? What will you be promoting? How long do you want the e-mail to be? Will you give it a name, like a newsletter? These are all things to consider when developing your content strategy, and this may overlap with other areas of content development such as your blog of social media channels.

Another consideration is how you will grow your e-mail list. You can include a signup form on your Web site, or you can promote your e-mail newsletter on social media. You can e-mail your current contacts to let them know you've started an e-mail list and ask if they would like to sign up. You can also ask for people to sign up when you give a workshop or presentation. It's best to always ask people to "opt in" to your e-mail list (and many e-mail marketing providers require that you do). Nobody wants to suddenly receive e-mail from a business if they didn't knowingly sign up for it. But a good strategy to use at workshops is to ask people to give their e-mail address if they want to receive your slides or handouts via e-mail. Then, in that e-mail you can direct them to sign up to continue to receive e-mail from you in the future.

UTILIZING SOCIAL MEDIA

Just as you need to be strategic about how you use e-mail marketing, you also need to be strategic about how you utilize social media channels to promote your independent consulting or freelancing business. You will likely want to use some social media to market yourself and build relation-ships, but which social media channels you use will depend on your brand, your marketing goals, the type of work you do, and which channels your target clients are using.

You shouldn't feel obligated to engage in all social channels; however, there are a few that prove to be most commonly used across the board. Even if you don't use social media for your personal life, you should strongly consider using a few channels for your business. One objection people often have to social media is that they lose some of their sense of privacy; how-ever, you can choose what information to share. This means you can choose to only share information that helps identify your brand, build your reputa-tion, and build relationships with current and potential customers.

LinkedIn

As a consultant or freelancer running your own business, a LinkedIn page is essential. LinkedIn is the go-to social network for work, business, and professional communication. Your LinkedIn profile should be the go-to place where you list your professional experience, qualifications, affiliations, project work, and description. When people search for your name in a search engine, your LinkedIn profile will be one of the top search results. If you do not have a LinkedIn profile, you are missing an opportunity for people to learn about what you do. Even worse, if you have a LinkedIn pro-file but it is out of date, you are sending a message that you are not actively using one of the most important social media profiles you have as a business owner. If you don't already have one, get a LinkedIn account. If you do get an account, keep it updated at least quarterly.

Beyond the basics, you can also use LinkedIn to create a business profile, generate and share content, and participate in online communities. Your business profile is separate from your individual profile. If you have a busi-ness name that is different from your name, then it is a good idea to also create a business page. This is also a good idea if you are part of a group of consultants under one firm or office. Once you have created a business page, you can post on behalf of the business or post on behalf of yourself.

LinkedIn allows you to create posts. Similar to e-mail marketing or blog-ging, this is a great way to generate credibility, talk about the services you provide, and communicate with colleagues. You can repost blogs or other content from your Web site, or you can create entirely new content. You will want to consider this when you develop your content strategy. LinkedIn posts also allow you to showcase your work to audiences outside of librar-ies. If you are a consultant who works with other fields outside of librarian-ship, you will definitely want to reach a wider audience. But even if you are solely focused on library work, there is a benefit to boosting your online presence to a wider audience. As other professionals outside of libraries read about your work, they will gain a better understanding of what libraries do and why they exist. Your presence helps boost public perception of the entire profession.

LinkedIn has user groups, some of which are active communities that use the space to discuss professional issues and ideas. Search for groups based on your areas of expertise and join them. This will give you the opportunity to network and learn from colleagues while you build your reputation.

Facebook

Another social network that is nearly essential for library-focused consultants and freelancers is Facebook. Facebook is still the most commonly used social media platform, with 79 percent of adults having a personal account (Greenwood, Perrin, & Duggan, 2016). The biggest concern users have with Facebook is privacy, and many people still do not want to use Facebook for work purposes. However, Facebook has developed many new tools for managing privacy settings. If this is of concern, you should take a look at how to set up specific groups so you either exclude professional colleagues from posts or only include them when you choose to do so. Although you shouldn't use your personal account solely to promote your business, chances are you will have professional contacts as Facebook friends. This is a good way to manage your privacy when it comes to professional contacts.

Create a Facebook page for your business, even if you are only working under your own name. This Facebook page is where you will post information only relevant to your work. People can "like" or "follow" your page in order to receive updates from you. You can purchase ads to promote your posts, and the rates are incredibly low for the return. At this point, it can be very difficult to build a Facebook audience without paying for ads, but even as little as five dollars per post can help reach a wider audience. You can add events, share links to articles, and create posts to engage your followers.

Another opportunity for Facebook engagement is through Facebook groups. These are online communities where individuals can discuss issues related to a common topic. Facebook groups give you an opportunity to engage with other library professionals, build credibility, and share your ideas. Some consultants use groups to have more in-depth discussion with their clients and followers. Others create groups to foster discussion on a topic of interest. Even if you don't create a group, you can always join groups created by others to have conversations on professional issues. There are a large number of library-specific Facebook groups, ranging from entirely casual to highly professional. Groups can be set to "private" or "secret" to hide the content from the public.

Twitter

Library consultants and freelancers should consider having an active Twitter account, but it isn't essential. However, there are circles of librarianship that are very active on Twitter, so having an account (even if you don't use it regularly) is a good idea. This also helps claim your brand identity on the social media platform should you decide to use it more actively later on.

Twitter is a social media community that tends to share resources, participate in conversations (sometimes formalized as Tweet Chats), and promote events. Twitter takes more cultivating. The more active you are on it, the more you will find others engaging with you. You will find that most library associations, libraries, and regional agencies are now using Twitter actively. Many high-profile librarians actively use Twitter. Most library conferences and events are now using conference hashtags to track conversations, so tweeting at a conference can be a great way to use Twitter on an occasional basis.

Although Twitter does have paid ads, there isn't as wide of an audience. However, you can set up analytics to track how far your tweets are going. If you have the time, Twitter is a worthwhile channel to pursue.

Instagram

If you do anything that is visual in nature, you should get an Instagram account specifically for your business as a consultant or freelancer. Instagram is a platform based entirely in images, especially photographs. If you travel for your work or you do graphic or visual design work, your Instagram can help you reach that particular audience. If you use Instagram personally and keep your profile public, you can leverage it for both personal and business uses. For example, if you travel occasionally for work, you can post pictures from your work travel in your personal Instagram account. People will likely know you by name, so this helps to expand your brand reach. One important thing to note with Instagram is that image quality is very important, so don't post an image if it is blurry or has bad lighting (unless you have some specific reason to do so). Instagram is an opportunity to showcase your best amateur photography skills.

SlideShare

Although not exclusively a "social" channel, SlideShare is an excellent way to share content from presentations, keynotes, and workshops that helps to showcase your work and build credibility. As a consultant or freelancer, you may not want to share all of your slide content, but you will want to share some of it. The best content to share is from any presentation that is already available to a wide audience. You may also want to share abbreviated versions of workshops that you are available for hire for. SlideShare is a part of LinkedIn, so if you have a LinkedIn profile, you can also post your SlideShare content there.

Other Social Media Channels

Many other social media channels are popular among smaller user groups with specific interests. If you are social media savvy, or if you are looking to reach specific audiences, you may consider platforms like Snapchat, Pinterest, Tumblr, Google+, or Reddit. The key to choosing any social media platform is really to identify why that platform will benefit your business, who you are trying to reach, and how you want to present your business (or yourself) on that particular platform.

General Social Media Tips

Regardless of which social media channels you choose, there are a few things you should keep in mind. Remember that people viewing on one (or several) channels are seeing only a slice of what you have to offer. These tips will help you have a consistent brand identity across all channels.

- Use the same photograph across all professional platforms. People will know you by your face online, so having the same photo on all platforms makes it easier for people to recognize you. If you use personal profiles for professional purposes, make sure to change those photos to match anytime you are going to a conference or event. And be sure to take new professional photos at least every two to three years. If you tend to change your hairstyle or color often, you may need to do this more frequently (Kawasaki, 2015, ch. 1).

- Think about what tone you want to present in all of your messaging and how that tone is representative of your personal brand. Tone can be conveyed in the words you choose, the choice to include emojis or .gifs, and the style of message that you post. Is your style as a consultant edgy or traditional? Is your target client a library director and what is their expectation of professionalism (and how do you meet that)? Do you share provocative ideas to push the envelope of librarianship, or do you stick to mainstream library news? Do you use formal language, or are you more casual? Think about what matches your brand identity and be true to it.

- Think about ways to cross-post content on multiple platforms, but do this strategically. Do you have a blog post to share? See if you can post it on Facebook one day, Twitter the next, and then LinkedIn the following week. You will be more likely to reach more followers if you rotate your content in this way. Even when reposting content from others, it pays to be strategic. You can use a social media calendar if you wish to track this formally, but you can also just take a few minutes each day to thoughtfully select new posts for each channel (or use a social media scheduler like HootSuite).

When you think about which social media platforms to use for your consulting or freelancing business, be strategic. Think about where you want to invest your time and how those channels will help you build your brand and reputation. If a social media channel doesn't serve your purpose, then don't use it. But if you choose to use a channel, do your best to use it to your advantage.

TARGETING MARKETING TO SPECIFIC AUDIENCES

When you create your marketing plan, you should think about who you are trying to reach. What organizations may want to contract you for the services you want to provide? Which individuals within those organizations have the authority to contract with you? And which individuals may also have influence on that decision or can engage with you during the process? If you are looking at marketing as a holistic and ongoing process, then you will want to think beyond just the organization or the purchasing authority. Once you have identified your target audience, you can think about how you will interact with those individuals, what type of messaging you will use, and how you will build a relationship with them over time.

If you are just getting started as a consultant or freelancer, you may want to start with people you already know. Is there anyone you've worked with in the past who you could reach out to? Make contact with colleagues and former project partners and let them know you are open for business. Ask if they might make a referral or introduction if they know anyone who might be in need of your services. Ask if they are willing to write a testimonial for your Web site! Sometimes the best leads for new business will come from people who already know you.

ENGAGING IN VOLUNTEERISM AND PROFESSIONAL ACTIVITIES

Another part of marketing is the exposure you get presenting at conferences and participating in professional activities. Many library consultants and freelancers come through professional or managerial experience in libraries. Even for those who do not have an ML(I)S, participation in volunteer professional activities, such as those offered through associations and user groups, may provide an opportunity to stay connected to the profession.

Although it is true that these activities give you exposure, it is also important to draw an ethical line between active and passive marketing. It may give you great exposure to chair a committee, present at a conference, or serve on a board. However, these are not appropriate venues for selling or pitching your services.

Many businesses, freelancers, and consultants participate in professional activities as a part of "giving back" to the profession. When you find yourself in this position, consider your mission, purpose, and values. Make sure your volunteerism is in alignment with your brand identity, and take the ethical high road when giving back.

Another consideration when doing volunteer work for the profession is to focus on activities that are in alignment with your interests and brand identity, and choose your projects wisely. When you are in control of your own schedule, it can be very easy to volunteer for too many projects.

MY EXPERIENCE VOLUNTEERING WITH PROFESSIONAL ASSOCIATIONS

I've always valued my involvement with professional associations, serving the profession as a volunteer. But when I decided to become a consultant I had to rethink my involvement. I love attending conferences and being involved, but I have to be careful not to overextend myself. A part of my personal "brand" is dedication to the projects I'm working on, and following through on responsibility. I soon realized that if I said "yes" to everything, I wouldn't be able to do a good job with any of the volunteer work.

Early on in my path as a consultant I took on small volunteer responsibilities—helping with social media for a small national conference, organizing webinars for an interest group at my state association, chairing a conference program committee for one of ALA's round tables. I loved the variety, but I wanted to get involved more deeply. This led me to run for office on the executive board of a group that is very closely tied to my work as a consultant: ALA's Learning Round Table. When I did this I decided to back off on other volunteer jobs so I could really focus on one particular area.

As I write this I'm in my second year of a three-year term, and I am so glad that I made the decision to scale back in other areas of service. I'm really able to devote my time to a group in a way that I find rewarding, and also where I am able to really help out. I also am able to network with others who do similar work, and learn from their experiences. I see this volunteer work as an extension of my professional activities, not as an opportunity to promote my business.

NETWORKING WITH OTHER PROFESSIONALS

As a consultant or freelancer, networking is a very important tool in your marketing plan. Whether at a conference reception or at a local professional meetup, networking is the way you build relationships with potential, current, and previous clients. Networking events are an opportunity for professional socializing.

Of course, you can't spend all your time networking, so you will need to identify which events will be the best opportunities. Here are some factors for you to consider:

- Which conferences should you attend to reach your ideal clients/customers?
- When attending a conference, which receptions and happy hours align with your brand identity? Which events relate to your work?
- If you have to choose between two events at the same time, which event will give you an opportunity to meet new people? Which will allow you to connect with your current network?
- How many networking events can you successfully attend in a day, week, or month? At what point do you become too tired to network effectively?

When you are networking, remember to stay true to yourself and to your brand. This is called authenticity, and is essential for any consultant or free-lancer. The goal of networking is not to impress other people or to act a certain way to gain the favor of others. The goal of networking is to get to know people and to let them get to know you. Of course, in a professional context we are still looking at presenting a professional image of ourselves, and that is where our brand can be our guide. Your professional personality is an authentic representation of yourself and is tied to the purpose and values of your work.

If you are new to networking or if you are not confident making conversation in networking environments, it may take time to get more comfortable. Similarly, if you consider yourself to be shy or introverted, you may find yourself avoiding networking events. However, networking is a skill that you can learn over time. The more you practice, the easier it will get. If you want to get better at networking, the best thing is to go out and get more experience. Attend local networking events and meetups so you can get more comfortable and become more aware. Remember that networking does not only have to apply to new connections, but can also be the act of continuing your current connections (Young Entrepreneur Council, 2012). The more you try, the easier it gets.

Whether you are a new networker or a seasoned socializer, it may help you to focus on a few of these networking tips:

1. Make eye contact with the person you are speaking to (Sweeney, 2015). It can be tempting to look around the room or to look away. However, when you don't make eye contact, you are missing an opportunity to build a relationship (and you may be giving off the impression that you are uninterested in the conversation or the person you are speaking with). Making eye contact is a nonverbal signal that you are interested in the conversation at hand and signifies that you are listening to the person speaking. It is an essential networking skill.

2. Remember to listen more than you speak (Sweeney, 2015). Networking shouldn't just be talking about you, but also asking others to talk about their interests. Take time to get to know other people (which takes the spotlight off yourself). Think of a few good conversation starters to ask at the event, such as "Tell me about the community your library serves . . ." or "How did you get involved with this group?"

3. A great conversation starter is to ask "What's a good book you've read recently?" This is a great topic for libraries, because books and literacy fuel so much of library work. It is a good idea to have your own response to this question as well, in case you are asked in return.

4. Think of a few examples that would make good conversations when asked "What are you working on?" Talking about just one project can help illustrate your work and can also make for interesting conversations. It is good to have a few examples to pull from so you can change it up from one conversation to the next.

5. Take a break when you're feeling overwhelmed or if you've been in the same conversation too long (Sweeney, 2015). Make a polite exit from the conversation to use the restroom, get a drink of water, or get a breath of fresh air. Then you can return after you've had a chance to recharge, and you can opt to mingle with a new group.

The next time you have a networking event to attend, start by observing your own natural tendencies without passing any judgment on yourself. Later on, reflect on your experience and identify one or two areas you'd like to improve and how you could focus on one small way to get better at that skill. Then try to remember that the next time you have a networking event.

CONCLUSION

Marketing is a combination of activities. It is an ongoing process, not a single event. It is as much about building relationships as it is about advertising your services. Successful marketing will result in you booking clients that align with your personal and professional goals. It is important to have a marketing plan, and it is also important that you continually revisit that plan and make adjustments as needed. There is no "formula" for marketing success. It takes having a thoughtful approach, knowing your target audience, and carefully choosing which activities to engage in with the resources you have available. Whatever approach you choose to take when it comes to marketing, remember that the most important thing is to remain true to your brand and to keep your values in focus as you communicate with current and potential clients about your work.

RESOURCES

Fine, Debra. The fine art of small talk: how to start a conversation, keep it going, build networking skills, and leave a positive impression! New York: Hachette Books, 2014.

Godin, Seth. "Define: Brand." *Seth's Blog*, December 13. http://sethgodin.typepad .com/seths_blog/2009/12/define-brand.html

Greenwood, Shannon, Andrew Perrin, and Maeve Duggan. "Social Media Update 2016." *Pew Research Center, November 11.* http://www.pewinternet.org/2016 /11/11/social-media-update-2016

Kawasaki, Guy. *The Art of Social Media: Power Tips for Power Users.* London: Penguin Books Ltd. Kindle, 2015.

Levinson, Jay Conrad, and Jeannie Levinson. *Guerrilla Marketing Remix: The Best of Guerilla Marketing* (Kindle version). Entrepreneur Press, 2011.

Merriam-Webster, Inc. *Merriam Webster's Collegiate Dictionary.* New York: Merriam-Webster, Inc., 2014.

Pinkham, Ryan. "10 Reasons to Use E-mail Marketing (as Told by Small Businesses)." *Forbes, September 27.* https://www.forbes.com/sites/constantcontact /2015/09/17/10-reasons-to-use-e-mail-marketing-as-told-by-small-businesses /#4ba453b58c03

Sernovitz, Andy. *Word of Mouth Marketing: How Smart Companies Get People Talking.* Greenleaf Book Group Press, 2012.

Sweeney, Patrick. "Schmoozing for Beginners." California Library Association Conference, Pasadena, CA, November 6–8, 2015. http://www.slideshare.net /pcsweeney/schmoozing-for-beginners

Wilson, Jeffrey S. "The Best Web Hosting Services of 2017." *PC Mag,* January 13. http://www.pcmag.com/article2/0,2817,2424725,00.asp

Young Entrepreneur Council. "16 Quick Tips to Become a Better Networker." *Forbes,* November 30. https://www.forbes.com/sites/theyec/2012/11/30/16-quick-tips-to -become-a-better-networker/#6b56646ad7f4

7

Pipelines and Charging for Services

Melissa Stockton, Quipu Group

This chapter covers information related to pipelines for new business, charging for consulting services, and when it can be best to decline a project. These are all areas that should be considered prior to beginning a consulting business and are also aspects of your business that will need to be evaluated on a regular basis.

PIPELINES

As with other contract-type professions, consulting requires that you work on current projects while keeping an eye toward the next project(s). Although it feels great to be busy and working on many different projects, you have to remember that the current projects will eventually come to an end. You need to make sure that the pipeline is as full as you need it, juggling current projects along with work on marketing and finding your next project. You should try to have as many projects as possible in your pipeline, getting some projects ready to proceed as soon as you are ready and also working on those projects that take a considerable amount of time to complete.

Cash flow, the money going in and out, is the main reason you need to keep a pipeline. Maintaining your pipeline allows you to exert some control over the "feast or famine" kind of existence that small businesses and consultants experience. Having projects in various stages of completion, or "in the pipeline," keeps the work, and money, coming in at a steady rate. Generally.

How Much in the Pipeline?

The number of items you need to have in the pipeline at any given time will vary. It will depend on the types of contracts you have and the monetary goals you have set for your business. Many things make it difficult to determine how many projects you need to have in your pipeline, and you need to get to know the flow of your own consulting work.

Some questions to ask yourself:

- How long do your projects last?
- How many of each type of project can you work on at one time?
- Which potential projects will require a lengthy contract?
- How many noncontract items do you have on your schedule (conferences, white papers, programs/webinars)?
- When do you want to take a vacation?

Knowing how long projects will take to complete is sometimes impossible. Delays on the client side are frequent and usually out of your control. Projects can also change in scope and complexity, which alters their overall timeline. Consultants offering training or other types of services that can be planned, scheduled, and executed according to a fairly straightforward plan still face potential issues and delays when people get sick or resign from their positions, money dries up, or not enough people sign up for a class. Consultants can also face delays due to changing priorities within the library. If you are working with a specific department when the library receives the money to build a new branch, you may have to wait until the building project is somewhat completed before any library staff has time to focus on other areas.

Contracts are an area that can also take longer than you might wish to complete. The first contract related to a project will be your contract for consulting work. Public libraries often need to go through their city or county purchasing department to complete any contracts. Consortia and other library-related organizations are often independent of any city or county government requirements. Even if it is not required, completing a city or county contract may be the quickest way for you to get through this stage of the hiring process. Depending on the complexity of the contract, you may want to utilize the services of an attorney to review any contract before you sign it. It is very common for contracts from city or county governments to include many odd clauses that would never come into play with consulting work. Unless you are working with a library on a new building or a remodel, you will probably never have to wear a hard hat while on the job!

You need to review any contract for payment processes and insurance requirements. Insurance requirements can include several types of insurance, including workers compensation, general liability, automobile liability, and errors and omissions. Having your own contract that can be offered to clients is a very good idea and often can be used if the dollar amount of the contract is low enough or when the client is not required to go through an official city or county procurement process.

When using your own contract or using a contract template from your customer, there will often be a need to have the document reviewed by attorneys on one or both sides of the arrangement. If the customer makes changes to your contract, you may need to run the changes by your own attorney. If you need to make any adjustments to a contract originating from your client, they will usually need to have their own attorneys review the changes. With any contract that requires an attorney to review it, you will need to assume two to five days for each review. Areas that often need to be adjusted are related to the location/state of any legal actions arising out of the contract, removing or waiving any workers compensation requirements, and modifications to other insurance requirements. So, if you begin with a contract provided by your client, you will need your attorney to review the document initially, and then your client will need to pass any changes by their own attorney, meaning there will be an additional 4 to 10 business days required just for the attorney reviews. The bottom line is that any time a contract needs to be reviewed by a legal entity—either your own or the client's—there may be some delay in signing.

It is best to expect that schedules and workloads will shift on a regular basis, so it is usually better to have too many future projects on your radar than too few.

How to Fill the Pipeline

There are a variety of different methods you can use to get new projects and to keep things in your pipeline. This section will cover responding to RFP/RFI/RFQs, word-of-mouth marketing, and repeat customers.

Responding to an RFP/RFI/RFQ

When an organization puts together a list of services required and asks for consultants to respond, it may take the form of a request for proposal (RFP), request for quote (RFQ), or a request for information (RFI). There are subtle differences depending on the letters used in the request. Often, an RFI is released and is the least stringent format. An RFQ and an RFP are almost synonymous and usually are the more binding types of requests, requiring a more complete proposal from the respondents. The information required to complete an RFP/RFI/RFQ response is basically the same, although an RFI may provide for more flexibility in the response. The type of request made by a client will usually be determined by the purchasing rules with which they must comply. The actual content of a response will be similar. The rest of this section references responses to RFPs. Because an RFP usually requires a complete proposal, the following will address all types of requests.

Responding to RFPs is not the easiest way to get business; however, for large jobs and some organizations, it is the only way they can procure your services. Going through an RFP process is definitely one way to put potential projects into your pipeline, but be aware that there is a longer lead-in time than with other methodologies. Respondents are usually given three to four weeks to respond to an RFP, and then the organization will take some time to review the responses and possibly interview candidates before a final decision is made. Responses to RFIs may have a shorter time period for submission and decision; however, they will also have fewer requirements for the proposals.

It is very important that you read through the RFP in detail as soon as you can. There may be requirements to get a business license with the city or to provide proof of insurance or other things that may take you some time to gather. There is usually a specific time period given for sending in questions related to the RFP, and you definitely don't want to miss the deadline for asking any questions or to get further clarification on the work that the client is expecting from the selected consultant.

Although every RFP is different, there are some sections that you usually find in every RFP. You can create boilerplate information that can be copied into every proposal with very little editing. You will want to customize this basic information so that it speaks directly to the project described in the RFP.

It is common for every RFP to include questions related to the following areas.

Professional Background and Related Experience

Some RFPs may ask for your resume, but they will all require you to describe your background and experience. Having an up-to-date resume is helpful, but you will also need to describe your qualifications in a way that is specifically related to the work requested in the RFP. It helps to be creative when describing your past experience and to highlight things that speak directly to the services described in the RFP. For example, if you previously managed a technical services department in a library and are responding to an RFP asking for a review of the workflow for an acquisitions process, you would not need to talk about how well you can catalog, but rather describe a time when you were involved in a workflow analysis or when you brought in a new vendor or a new system that helped you streamline the processes in technical services.

References

Be prepared to provide references for your work. The more closely the references relate to the work being requested in the RFP, the better. For example, if you are responding to an RFP for a library consortium, whenever possible, use other consortia as references. As always, ask each client or former employer if they are willing to be a reference for you and then keep up with those folks. Send them a copy of the RFP so they are aware of the project you are applying for. People move positions and get new jobs in new locations, and you need to be able to give current contact information for each person you include in your proposal. If your references have moved to a new position or a new organization, if they are willing, you can continue to use them in your proposals. Just include a note indicating their relationship to the previous workplace at which you worked with them.

Scope of Work

Some RFPs will include a scope of work. This is a statement that describes the tasks required for the completion of a project. Others may include a scope of work that just describes the issues that the organization is trying to address. Your response should show an understanding of the work being requested, and it is good to include your own project plan for accomplishing the stated goals. Describe each phase or step of the project and make it very clear how the issues will be addressed and resolved. For each phase of your project plan, include a description of the work that will be done, an estimated time for completion, and the deliverable(s) that the client can expect from you. The client will expect you to follow your project plan and to provide the stated deliverables, so be careful that you don't promise more than you can do or more than is needed to complete the project. Deliverables can include things such as status reports, final reports, survey results, training, software, etc.

Pricing

Once you have determined your pricing model(s) (covered later in this chapter), use that information to complete the price quote for an RFP. You need to think about each project phase and what types of charges would be required. Will you be bringing other consultants or assistants into the project? What phases will require you to travel and see the client in person? How much time will each deliverable take you to create? RFPs do not usually include information on how much the client is willing or able to spend, so your pricing needs to balance the total cost of the project with a good idea of how much time and resources will be required from you. It is often a good idea to offer options in the price quote; for example, you may want to include pricing options for onsite meetings as well as virtual meetings. Travel is usually a very expensive part of any bid, and providing options in this area can be very helpful.

Timelines

You may find that an RFP includes an unreasonable time frame for the work that needs to be accomplished. This should not stop you from responding, even if you do not feel you can complete the project in the time allotted. You can provide them with information on when you could start the project and give them your opinion on how long you believe it will take to complete. In a way, this can be the start of the consulting service by giving the client a more reasonable expectation of the time that will be involved in completing the work they are requesting.

Whenever possible, try to talk with the people who released the RFP. There are often rules that preclude you from talking to the people you will be working with; however, it always helps to have someone describe their needs in a conversation. In the RFP, a person will be named as the contact for the proposal. Use the information provided to contact the appropriate person and ask if you can have a conversation with people in the organization who will be involved in the project. This request may be denied depending on how strict the RFP process is handled. If you are unable to have a conversation with the parties that will be involved in the actual project, you should be able to put together a list of questions that will be responded to in writing. The questions you ask during this time, whether in person or in writing, should clarify the project goals and ensure that you are addressing the real needs of the client. The more you know about the issues and the ultimate result the client is looking for, the better proposal you will be able to create. For more on projects and project management, see Chapter 8 by Emily Clasper.

Getting the Word Out

Once you provide consulting services to one library or group in a region of the United States, you may then get a number of other requests from other organizations in the area. Librarians talk to each other! They ask people they know how they handled a situation or filled a need and will follow the path that is presented to them. When you complete a project and the client is happy, it is very possible that you will receive a number of calls for the same services.

As covered in many previous chapters, especially Crystal Schimpf's chapter on marketing and networking, as a consultant you need to network and continuously add to your network. This helps to make sure that there are people working in the field who know you and know at least something about the services you offer. Going to conferences and meetings related to your area of expertise is a great way to get to know more people. If you attend a program, don't be afraid to speak up! You might end up getting a job because of a comment or question you asked during a presentation.

Figure out if there are any topics you know in depth that you could put into a presentation. Giving presentations at a conference offers you a chance to talk to people who are specifically interested in your area of knowledge. Presenting a program on your own is good; however, it is always better if you can present a program with a client or other working librarians, especially if it is on a successful project you completed with a client. It is great for your resume and may open up a variety of opportunities for you while you are helping libraries by sharing your knowledge. You have a unique perspective because you work with a variety of libraries and see many different ways a single problem has been solved by libraries. Just sharing the experiences you have had with different environments is very helpful to the working librarian.

Writing an article with other librarians or clients is a great way to show your worth as well. Working librarians love to see how other people have solved a problem or completed a project. Then, when they decide to hire a consultant, they think of you.

Getting to know other consultants and understanding what services they offer is another avenue that can bring in business. When a library uses a consultant for a project, they often will contact that consultant when they have another project—no matter what the topic or area of expertise. Being able to recommend other consultants not only allows you to help your client, but may also provide you with the ability to partner with other consultants to expand the type and complexity of projects you can complete. Although there is some competition in the world of library consulting, it is certainly not the cutthroat world you will find in other types of businesses. It is best to look at other library consultants as potential partners rather than just competition.

The Association of Specialized and Cooperative Library Agencies (ASCLA), a division of the American Library Association (ALA), supports the Library Consultants Interest Group. This interest group does morph and change on a regular basis; however, they have sponsored "Consultants Give Back" sessions at the ALA annual conference for a number of years. These sessions offer a half hour of free consulting to anyone attending the conference. The librarians who use this service are sometimes from libraries that cannot afford to hire a consultant, but are also often librarians at the beginning of a large project who are just trying to figure out what all they need to think about before getting started. For the consultants, you not only get to hear about some interesting projects from the participants, but you also get to meet other consultants and learn more about what types of consulting options are possible.

The Web site libraryconsultants.org is another inexpensive way to get your name out into the library world and to let people know about your consulting work. This is a website that contains profiles for library consultants and enables library staff to see the areas of expertise and some example projects for each consultant listed.

Repeat Clients

The feasibility of having repeat clients for your consulting services depends on the type of consulting services you provide. Consultants who provide training or staff enrichment services are often able to maintain a regular client base, whereas those who provide help with new buildings or new systems do not provide services that are required on a regular basis. If you have not already learned this, you need to know that the library world has a long memory, and it is never a good idea to burn any bridges! As covered in

Chapter 2 by Carson Block, getting and maintaining clients is not difficult if you are honest about your knowledge and skills and provide the best service possible to each client. If you are indeed good at what you do, repeat clients can automatically happen.

If you do provide services that are not constantly in demand for a single client or library, it is still a good idea to keep in touch with your clients. You may need to use them as references, and they provide a good method for gauging how well you are doing your job. Finding out how things go after your project is done will help you figure out if you need to change your methods or add new options for future clients. Maintaining contact with your clients and meeting for coffee or lunch at conferences or when you are in their area goes a long way to keeping the relationships fresh and keeping your name in the front of their minds. For more on customers and where to find them, see Pat Wagner's Chapter 3.

CHARGING FOR SERVICES

As a consultant, you are not selling widgets or databases to libraries, but you are selling your expertise and need to know and understand what value your services give to libraries. When you work in a service industry and with organizations that are traditionally underfunded, it can be difficult to set your pricing. Although a full pipeline can help to keep the cash flow solid, if you don't charge enough, then there will never be enough time in your schedule to complete the number of projects or contracts that will keep your mortgage paid. Libraries are well known for using the chorus "we have no money;" however, it is amazing how many of them seem to be able to find money for things they really want or need. In the past, many areas of the country provided libraries with enough of a budget to sustain services but also a large amount of discretionary funds. This is no longer the case; the multiple economic crises and dips have made libraries much more accountable for every dollar they spend. Having a regular pricing schedule allows you to respond more quickly to requests for quotes and gives you at least one thing you do not have to rethink for every potential project.

Overhead is what is used to cover indirect expenses for your business. In consulting, travel costs, printing, and other expenses are direct expenses that are expended for a specific project or client. Overhead expenses are indirect and include items such as rent, insurance, telephone, and other items used to run your business.

Overhead is usually referred to as a percentage of sales. Select a time period for determining your overhead—you may want to do this on a monthly or quarterly basis. Divide your monthly overhead cost by monthly sales and multiply by 100 to find the percentage of overhead cost. For example, if the sales for one month is $10,000 and the overhead costs for that month are $2,500, then $2,500/$10,000 * 100 = 25%.

Here are some of the overhead expenses that you may have for a consulting business:

- Telephone—cell, conference service, fax machine or service
- Web site
- Webinar software
- Office space (home or other)
  - Furniture
  - Utilities
  - Insurance
- Office supplies (paper, staples, postage, etc.)
- Equipment
  - Printer
- Health insurance
- Auto insurance
- Business insurance—general liability, errors and omissions
- Legal assistance
- Financial software
- Financial services
- Taxes

You need to have a variety of pricing options available, depending on the types of consulting services you provide. Coming up with your regular hourly or daily rate is difficult, but it is more difficult to figure out how much time any given project will take. Unless you offer a very specific course or training program, every consulting project will be a little different and require you to guess at the resources you will need to expend to complete it. You get better at this with experience; however, as mentioned in previous chapters, there are so many factors involved in many consulting projects that there is no way for you to know what challenges you will face.

Pricing Models to Think About

Hourly/Daily

You will need to determine an hourly and a daily rate for your services. Your hourly rate may seem high; however, you must remember that you will never be able to bill every hour of your workday and you need to cover things like getting a new computer or phone, paying for your healthcare, and other overhead costs. Once you have completed several consulting projects, you will be able to more closely match your hourly rate to the total amount of income you need each year. Your daily rates need to take into consideration that you will be providing committed time to the project and will not be available to other clients during the day. Be aware that charging, and especially invoicing, a project based on hourly charges can be time consuming. Not only do you have to keep track of the time you spend working; you must keep track of this information, provide it on invoices, and keep up with the total number of hours you have put into the project overall.

Project/Bid

Another form of pricing is by project. You may even be asked to do so by an RFP. Some clients will want a breakdown of how you determine this project cost, whereas others will simply want a single dollar figure. Even if you only need to provide a single dollar figure, it would be helpful if you created a detailed list of the activities you have planned for completing the project. If you need to negotiate with the client, your list will help you determine where you can cut costs without hurting your bottom line.

When possible, it is helpful to include specific phases or milestones within a project. This not only helps you and the client see how much has been done and what else needs to happen; it also allows you to split up your invoicing so that you can invoice in increments and not wait until a project is completed before you get any payments. You may want to include a "kick-off" or a project launch type of phase at the beginning of the project, which will bring some money in at the start. The "kick-off" phase can be used to review work that has already been done by the client in the project area, determine the key people involved in the process, provide a basic introduction for the consultant to the group, and finalize the project plan and timeline. It is also customary to ask for 20 percent to 50 percent of the total project cost at the beginning and then use the milestones or phases set out in the project plan to indicate the invoices that will be submitted throughout the life of the project.

Retainer

A retainer is an agreement between the consultant and the client that specifies the number of hours and the price per hour for the agreed-upon time period. Some types of consulting lend themselves to a retainer type of situation. Consultants providing training services offer a very easy-to-understand type of retainer situation. A library may pay a consultant/trainer a retainer for 10 hours of training each month for six months or a year. The specific type of training and the number of actual courses offered each month would be customized for the needs of the library; however, the retainer for those 10 hours a month would be automatically billed to the client. Consultants who offer coaching could also easily fit into a retainer type of situation. This may not be feasible for many consultants; although, it is a great way to know that you will have a specific amount of money coming to you on a regular basis. Many consultants are hired for specific projects that may not lend themselves to a retainer situation. For example, if you help libraries work through specific types of procurement activities, this would not be something libraries do on a regular basis. Retainers can definitely help reduce the feast or famine part of any small business.

Travel

There are a variety of ways that you can charge for travel, and you may need to be flexible and use different methods with different clients. Two acceptable methods are to charge hourly prices plus travel expenses and to have a travel pricing schedule.

Hourly Plus Travel Expenses   With this method, you can charge your regular hourly/daily rates for the hours you spend onsite and then bill the client for the exact amount of your actual travel expenses. This is very helpful when you travel to more expensive parts of the country, and it means that you do not have to figure in flight and hotel expenses into your project budget. If you are able to drive to the client location, you can charge them for mileage or you can charge them for the time it takes to drive to/from the site. The downside is that you do have to turn in the receipts for every part of the travel (flight, hotel, car, meals) and often will be required to follow the travel rules set out by the client. This can be difficult if you are working with a number of clients and each has their own set of rules for paying travel expenses. For example, some clients cannot pay for alcoholic beverages so if you want to have wine with dinner, you would need to pay for those items separately. Some clients may have a specific per diem for meal or hotel costs, and you will need to know the specific amounts allowed in these areas for each client. If you need to purchase personal items such as toothpaste or mouthwash, these would be things you would need to pay for yourself and not include in your charges for your client.

Travel Pricing Schedule   This method requires that you come up with a cost for onsite visits that includes the costs for your flight, hotel, car, and meals. You quote a specific amount for each day onsite and can also add an extra cost for the days you are actually traveling to and from the site. You will want to add a half-day of travel on each side of the trip because it does usually take at least a half a day to get from one place to another, particularly when you are flying.

Pricing Summary

Whether you price your services by the project or by the hour, you just need to make sure that you are able to cover all of your expenses. Using a single project bid may be appropriate for some situations, especially those that require you to respond to an RFP/RFQ/RFI, whereas hourly or daily pricing may be best for others. You can decide what is the most comfortable and logical for you and start with your favorite method; you just have to be ready to negotiate and change your method if it does not work for a specific client or a specific project. Pricing for travel is just the same—you should have your own favorite method for covering travel expenses, yet always be open to following the rules set out by a client.

WHEN AND HOW TO SAY NO

Saying "no" to a project may be one of the most difficult things you will ever have to do. It can be easier if you do not quite have the skill set that is required for the project; however, this is not the only reason to refuse a contract. It is important that you be honest with yourself and to understand your strengths and weaknesses well enough to know when you are not the right person for a specific consulting project. It is also important that you recognize your capacity and not overextend yourself—this just makes for a frustrating project for both you and your client. Because jobs may be slow in coming at the beginning of your consulting career, you might get used to taking on anything that comes your way. It can almost be exciting when you get to the point where you can say "no" to a project and not affect your bottom line.

Consulting works best when there is a good match between the client and the consultant. Every consultant is different, every person in the world has a unique personality, and every organization has its own special environment. Methodologies and levels of flexibility can also be important pieces in finding the right match.

Many consultants will look back at a project and say, "I should have known not to take that job . . ." but that is usually after the job is completed and after they have expended many more resources than they had planned for a project. If you are uncomfortable with a new consulting possibility in any way, make sure you examine your reasons. For example, if you have extreme trouble communicating with the client during the first contacts, you may want to give some serious thought into providing the organization with information about other appropriate consultants instead of taking on the job yourself. Having the wisdom to know when to say "no" to a project may be something you attain with experience.

Here are some things that may be "red flags" and should at least make you think twice about accepting a contract with a library.

Bad experiences with other consultants. When in initial conversations, the director or main contact describes multiple situations with consultants in the past that have been unsatisfactory. Not all consultants are good at what they do; however, if you know a consultant with whom the library has had problems in the past, it would be good to at least contact the consultant for some further details.

Timelines. When timelines provided by the client are unrealistic, your first step will be to contact the client to discuss the issue. Once you have explained your reasons for needing a longer timeline for a project, if the client is not willing or able to adjust the request, you should expect to be held to the unreasonable timeline if you take the contract.

Toxic environment. If you are looking at a consulting project that is meant to help the library staff work more collegially, if the administration of the library make it clear that they do not value their staff or the capabilities of their staff—watch out. If the administration does not change their perceptions and methods of handling the staff, there is not much chance your work will be given a chance to meet the stated goals.

Hurry up and wait. When putting together a consulting project with a client, you both should expect a reasonable turnaround when reviewing documents, creating project plans, and finalizing a contract. If you find that a potential client never communicates in a timely fashion yet insists on immediate responses from you, do not be surprised if this is the case throughout the life of the project. If you have a large number of projects going on at any given time, an immediate response to one client will not be possible and can be detrimental to all of your clients.

CONCLUSION

In order to maintain a business, you must have positive cash flow. As a consultant, you can help to maintain this cash flow by keeping a pipeline of future business and by charging clients the right amount—which is a balance between the value of the services you provide and the amount you need to live. Repeat clients and those potential customers that do not require you to go through an RFP/RFQ/RFI process to secure a consulting job will be ones you can move more quickly through the pipeline, from potential business to confirmed business. When, as a consultant, you need to create an official proposal to an RFP/RFQ/RFI, the timeline between initial contact and a signed contract for consulting services will be longer. Keeping your pipeline as full as possible is one of the best ways to ensure that you will be able to consistently bring in revenue.

Keep your pipeline full!

- Short- and long-term prospects
- Respond to RFP/RFQ/RFIs
- Repeat customers
- Word-of-mouth marketing

Maintaining a preferred pricing model will help you to quickly and effectively respond to requests for your services. Pricing by the project and providing hourly and daily pricing options are all accepted methods for charging for consulting services. Covering travel costs is another aspect of your pricing plan that should be thought out ahead of time. Consistent pricing methodologies will save you time when responding to potential clients; however, being flexible and able to meet the pricing needs of each client is more important.

Finally, there are times when you should say "no" to a project. This is something that is very difficult for many consultants but is made easier when projects are beyond your capabilities and/or expertise. Saying "no" in the right way can often help your reputation and will definitely mean that you will not have projects that are too big or too difficult for your skill set.

FURTHER READING

Beich, Elaine. *The Consultant's Quick Start Guide: An Action Plan for Your First Year in Business.* Jossey-Bass/Pfeiffer, 2001.

Block, Peter. *Flawless Consulting: A Guide to Getting Your Expertise Used.* Jossey-Bass, 2011.

Lorette, Kristie. *How to Open & Operate a Financially Successful Consulting Business.* Atlantic Pub. Group, 2010.

Merron, Keith. *Consulting Mastery: How the Best Make the Biggest Difference.* Berrett-Koehler Publishers, 2005.

Sandlin, Eileen F. *Start Your Own Consulting Business.* Jere L. Calmes, 2010.

Weiss, Alan. *Great Consulting Challenges and How to Surmount Them: Powerful Techniques for the Successful Practitioner.* Jossey-Bass/Pfeiffer, 2003.

Weiss, Alan. *Getting Started in Consulting.* 3rd edition. John Wiley & Sons, 2009.

Weiss, Alan. *Million Dollar Consulting: The Professional's Guide to Growing a Practice.* McGraw-Hill, 2009.

8

Getting It Done: Project Management Tips for Library Consultants

Emily Clasper, Suffolk Cooperative Library System

Learning about project management principles and methods is one of the most helpful things you can do to enhance your effectiveness as a library. Consulting is all about doing projects. Often, it involves the coordination and execution of many individual projects at the same time. Having a strong background in project management can be an invaluable asset, giving a consultant many tools that help make projects more successful. Using principles and techniques borrowed from project management as defined by the Project Management Institute (PMI) can enhance your skills as a consultant and help you more effectively face the challenges of getting many complex projects completed and helping your library clients toward even greater success.

PROJECT MANAGEMENT METHODOLOGIES

In order to effectively choose project management tools to help your latest project succeed, it's important to understand the characteristics of the most common project management methodologies. There are many, many "flavors" of project management, each designed to handle different kinds of projects and to solve a variety of problems. Some of the most popular project management methodologies include:

- **Waterfall**—This approach, also known as "traditional" project management, focuses on establishing a sequence of events that must occur in order to ensure project success. This sequence begins in the initiation and planning phases, then continues through project execution and quality assurance, and finally ending with a closing process (including acceptance of deliverables). The beginning of the waterfall approach focuses on defining project requirements, and changes to the carefully constructed plan are discouraged. This methodology is often used to manage projects with a clearly designed result, and a relatively predictable set of resources and conditions exists.

- **Agile**—The Agile approach is based on the concept of adaptability within continually changing situations. It relies heavily on constant, consistent feedback and is well suited to projects where the client needs to be part of the development of a deliverable. Agile methodologies are often used when developing software, user interfaces, or documentation.

- **Scrum Methodology**—Scrum is a form of Agile project management that produces work in short time cycles of activity called "sprints." This iterative approach is highly effective for projects that do not have strictly defined project requirements and the definition of the ultimate product is in flux. This approach relies heavily on effective collaboration between team members and stakeholders and does not usually rely on a traditional project manager "running the show."

- **Critical Path**—This methodology uses elements of waterfall and Agile approaches, but shifts the overall focus to resource management rather than tasks and schedules. In this methodology, a set of core elements is defined for the project (the critical chain or critical path), and the completion of these elements determines the project's minimum timeline. Project managers using the critical path method assign resources to the critical path to control the progress of the overall project, while simultaneously assigning resources to complete noncritical path tasks at the same time. This is a very effective way of ensuring a project is completed on time, but depends on having a lot of resources at hand, all of whom have the appropriate skill set.

- **The Rest**—Other project methodologies such as PRiSM, PRINCE2, spiral, Lean, event chain, and Kanban offer slightly different ways of managing projects and reaching goals, often being designed for projects within a specialized area such as healthcare, manufacturing, construction, or software development. Each of these approaches offers valuable tools for keeping projects on track and headed for success.

Because of the variable nature of the projects consultants typically work on, there is generally no "one size fits all" solution. Most successful projects can benefit greatly from incorporating elements of several methodologies into the process and choosing only the techniques and practices that fit well with the project and client. Having a solid knowledge of the most popular and effective methods of project management can give a consultant an arsenal of tools to draw from when solving the unique problems they may encounter.

PROJECT MANAGEMENT SUPERSTAR TACTICS

Regardless of the methodology (or combination of methodologies) you choose to use in tackling your next consulting project, there are a number of areas where borrowing concepts and techniques from project management can be invaluable. Four areas of project management recommended for consultants to focus on are:

1. Setting the stage
2. Project scope
3. Scheduling
4. Communication

Setting the Stage

Before the *real* work of working as a consultant for an organization can begin, it's a good idea to gather some information about the preexisting factors that may affect your project with the library. Libraries hiring consultants may be specific on the goals and requirements of the project you'll be working on with them (although this is sometimes not the case!), but they often don't think to provide additional information about the organization itself and the stakeholders you will be dealing with. Taking the time to delve deeper into getting to know your client and how they operate can help you choose the more effective methods for getting the project work done on time, within budget, and up to your professional standards. This can also provide a good opportunity to define and establish your role with the stakeholders involved in the project, as you will have a better sense of how the established team operates and has done things in the past.

PMI recommends focusing on two areas to gain this knowledge and form a basis for planning strategies and managing the execution of your project. The first of these is the *Organizational Process Assets (OPAs)*, or the repository of information and data that has been collected by an organization from past projects (Fremouw, 2011). OPAs might include documents, policies, procedures, plans, templates, guidelines, lessons learned, earned value, historical data and information, estimating, and risk assessments from past projects your client organization has completed. These documents and records are extremely valuable as a source of insight into how the organization has handled projects in the past, giving you clues about what to expect when embarking on your project with them.

In consulting with libraries, most clients do not object to sharing documentation from past projects to help get the current one started and are very willing to discuss the way things have been done in the past. It is especially valuable to get a sense of what went wrong (or not as well as planned) during past projects. Identifying past project pain points will help you and the client avoid making the same mistakes again, with the hope that each successive project will have fewer of the same kind of problems. Stakeholders in library projects are usually more than willing to share the pitfalls they have encountered in the past and are eager to avoid them in similar projects.

Another important thing to take a good hard look at as a consultant about to embark on a new project with an organization is what PMI terms *Enterprise Environmental Factors (EEFs)*. These are defined as "internal and external environmental factors that can influence a project's success, including: organizational culture, organizational structure, as well as the internal and external political climate" (Fremouw, 2011). This is the part where you get to know all of the key stakeholders, the personalities you will be dealing with, conflicts and power struggles between stakeholders, and the overall culture of the organization. You need to go into a project with a good understanding of how each of the key stakeholders is involved or affected by the project and what their role is both within the project, as well as within the organization in general.

Almost every library consultant has stories about the mistakes they've made in dealing with clients because they did not have enough knowledge of the EEFs. You don't want to find yourself in the position one library consultant did when she made the mistake of remarking on the apparent failure of the last project the library had undertaken in this area without realizing she was speaking to the very person who had heavily invested herself into planning and executing that disastrous project. It took this consultant a while to recover from that slip up, as the person in question took great offense at the comment. Fortunately, things were later smoothed over by discussing the positive points of the last project, and both parties worked together to find ways to incorporate "more of that" into the current undertaking. Having a more solid knowledge ahead of time of the EEFs she was dealing with would have saved this consultant a lot of trouble and embarrassment.

When taking on a consulting job, try to make as many opportunities as possible for "fact finding" about the organization and its main stakeholders. Ask the organization's leadership directly if they will share any OPA documents right at the start so that you can get a quick sense of how projects are handled there. In addition, set up phone calls or face-to-face meetings with people from the organization well ahead of the project start so you can ask formal questions and look for informal clues about the OPAs and EEFs. Many times, it is the nonverbal cues and informal stories over coffee that help you get the best sense of the organization and its players. And whenever possible, reach out to your network of library colleagues not affiliated with the organization in question to see if they have any insight into the culture and dynamics of the library you are set to work with. You can get extremely valuable insights from friends and colleagues who are outsiders with a loose connection to the library.

Creating a stakeholder register as early in the process as possible is a good way to ensure that you have considered all of the players in the scenario, along with some of their needs and their interest in the process. Once a list of the stakeholders has been compiled for the project, it is a good idea to consider a number of things for each person or group of people on the list:

- **What is their role in the project overall?**
- Are they doing some of the work? Are they consuming the product? Are they financing the project?
- **What is their level of impact on the project's success?**
- Will the success of the project depend on their contribution and to what degree?
- **What is the level of impact the project will have on them?**
- Is this an important part of their daily routine? Is this something they will need help adapting to?
- **What are the best ways to communicate with this stakeholder or stakeholder group?**
- Do these people ever check their e-mail? Is individual face-to-face communication appropriate? Is it okay if they find out information by reading the library newsletter?

Create the stakeholder register in a spreadsheet so that you can add columns to answer these questions, making it easy to add stakeholders who emerge later in the project or edit the information if needed. The end result is a handy all-in-one guide to the people involved in the project. The completed stakeholder register can form the basis for other project documents, such as the communication plan, or provide inputs for planning tools.

Another great tool to use while getting a project established is the *RACI matrix*. This is a chart that shows each stakeholder's role in the major parts of a project, rating them as Responsible (R), Accountable (A), Consulted (C), or Informed (I) in each aspect. Those responsible will actually be expected to do the work for that part of the project, whereas accountable stakeholders are the people who will ultimately bear accountability for the outcome of that work. Consulted stakeholders give input into the element of the project, although they may not be directly involved in doing the work. Stakeholders listed as informed (this would usually be everyone!) will at least be kept "in the loop" about what is going on with that portion of the project. Stakeholders may fall into multiple RACI designations, depending on the project and what is required of the project team members.

An example of a partial RACI Matrix is shown in Figure 8.1.

Completing a matrix like this provides a tool for creating a communication plan for the project, establishing stakeholder expectations, and reinforcing the roles of each stakeholder group. In libraries stakeholders

	Project Charter	Project Goals	Project Objectives	Software Selection	Software Installation	Software Testing	Training
Director	A	A	A	A	I	I	A
Project Manager	R	R,A	R,A	R	R,A	A	A
Team Member 1				R	R	R	R
Team Member 2				R	I	R	R
Team Member 3				C	I	R	R
Circulation Staff		C	C	C	I	R	R
Reference Staff	C	C	C	C	I	R	R
Community Groups	C	C	I	I	I	I	I
Board Members	A	I	I	I	I	I	I
General Community					I		I

FIGURE 8.1. Sample Raci Matrix

often enter into projects with an expectation that everyone will be consulted about everything. This is not always a reasonable expectation, and the level of involvement and responsibility that is expected from each stakeholder during the various phases of the project is best established early on.

As project management is a "people-centered" discipline, its tools are often an apt match for consultants, who must necessarily cultivate their interpersonal relationship skills. As a library consultant, you will be working to solve problems with organizations operating within their own little ecosystems. Getting as full a sense as possible of how those ecosystems operate, who's who on the food chain, and which stakeholders are the apex predators will help you establish your own place and set you up to make decisions that will create a stronger chance of project success.

Project Scope

Project scope is one of the most essential concepts to understand in project management. Mistakes on defining and maintaining the scope of a project can be disastrous for a project. But establishing a clear, attainable scope and keeping the project activities within that scope can create a stable foundation to build an amazing project on. Besides providing a basis for project planning, setting a concrete scope at the beginning of a project also gives a consultant an important tool for drawing up a contract for the job and giving the client a price quote.

To define the project's scope, you must begin by defining the goals of the project, as well as a set of measurable, attainable objectives. Beginning a project without a clear understanding of the ultimate purpose for undertaking it can easily lead to disaster. A good way to start is by leading prospective clients through a process of defining goals and objectives *before* taking a consulting job. This allows you to get a firm understanding of what they want to achieve and helps to set expectations for the work to be done. Beginning with a list of goals and objectives agreed upon by both parties ensures that everyone is on the same page from the start and reduces the chances of needing to redo any work later on.

With goals and objectives in place, a consultant can work with their client to define the deliverables for the project and establish a set of requirements for these deliverables. In short, the consultant and client need to agree on what, exactly, needs to be built in order to sufficiently address the goals and objectives, and what the client wants the product to look like. There are times when the client will come to you with their requirements already defined, but even then the consultant should assess these requirements carefully before committing to something you may ultimately be unable to deliver.

A complete list of deliverables and their requirements allows a consultant or project manager to develop a complete list of tasks that must be performed in order to produce the correct products over the course of the project. This task list can then be correlated with the available resources (such as time, budget, materials, and staff work) to create a project schedule and plan. The task list itself, along with the list of deliverables and their requirements, determines the scope of the project.

Before beginning work on the actual project tasks, your client will need to approve the scope and its component parts. This approval is usually part of the contract process, as the consultant and client agree on the work to be done. Once both parties have agreed on the established scope, the project work can begin.

Consultants need to be vigilant when it comes to staying within the project scope. Library culture is extremely service oriented, with a cultural emphasis on "going above and beyond" for customers. Consequently, library clients often expect a consultant to do the same when working for them. Exceeding expectations and providing amazing customer service is commendable; however, performing additional tasks not necessary to the completion of the project as agreed upon can lead to a downward spiral in terms of productivity and quality. There are times when going "above and beyond" for your client is a slippery slope toward blowing up your scope.

One common scope killer is the phrase "while we're at it." The creativity and enthusiasm of library professionals often lead them to dream of bigger and better outcomes while a project is already underway. Unfortunately, these kinds of suggestions are usually outside the scope of the project, and although they would be nice to incorporate, doing so could result in the dreaded "scope creep." Adding things on can easily throw the schedule off, strain the budget, or overtax the people doing the work. As a consultant, they can cost you in time, cause you to do free work, and may be detrimental to your reputation if the rest of the project and its results are negatively affected.

Although the passion library workers bring to their projects and the imagination they apply to solving problems is wonderful, consultants often find themselves in the position of bringing them back down to Earth and the realities involved with getting the work at hand completed on time, on budget, and on schedule. This doesn't mean that the "while we're at it" add-ons weren't great ideas . . . but maybe not for this project. Consultants who find themselves working with extremely zealous staff who often like to propose project changes that could unintentionally sabotage the rest of the project may want to come up with strategies ahead of time to handle this situation.

One common tactic within the project management discipline is the implementation of a formal change management process for the project. This means that when the consultant and client agree on the scope of the project, they also agree on a procedure for proposing changes to the scope, deliverables, schedule, and requirements. Often this takes the form of requiring a formal change request to be filed, generally through the submission of a change request form. The request is then reviewed by a preestablished group of people, including the consultant and the stakeholders ultimately accountable for the project outcomes and keeping the project on budget.

A formal review process ensures that no additional unnecessary tasks are incorporated into the project, thereby increasing risk. It also ensures that there is a formal record of the suggestion, which can be filed for consideration as part of a future project. Great ideas shouldn't get discarded outright just because they don't fit the immediate project at hand. Encourage your clients to keep track of the suggestions their staff offer during the project, even if you can't get to them right away. Maybe there's another project down the line that the suggestion will be a perfect fit for. And hopefully you've done a good enough job on this current project to get hired again for that future one.

The project scope is your ultimate guide to what needs to be done and what it needs to look like when it's finished. If you stick to the project scope, doing no more and no less than necessary to meet the requirements outlined there, you will, in theory, accomplish the objectives and goals of the project using the fewest resources. Staying efficient while being effective relies on a clearly defined project scope that is adhered to throughout the project. It saves the client and the consultant time, money, and effort, while keeping the standards for the project high.

Scheduling

Few things are more important to the successful completion of a project than the schedule. Scheduling a project is a complex activity dependent on many fluctuating variables. Each project has unique factors to take into consideration when creating the schedule. Consequently, there are many different methods for creating a project schedule, depending on the methodology used to manage the project and unique factors affecting this specific project. Most project scheduling processes, however, incorporate some variation of the following steps:

1. Define activities—As mentioned earlier in this chapter, the deliverables and requirements can be used to create a comprehensive list of tasks to be performed in order to successfully meet the desired outcomes. Creating this list of activities is the first step in most project planning processes.

2. Sequence activities—Once a project manager knows what needs to be done, the next step is to determine what order to do the tasks in. This is usually an exercise in common sense, as there is usually a logical sequence for the tasks of any given project.

3. Determine dependencies—Often performed simultaneously with sequencing, the project manager needs to establish which tasks are dependent on others. For instance, installing carpeting is dependent on laying the subflooring, and computer terminals cannot be installed until the workstations are in place.

4. Estimate resources—During this step, the project manager assesses the people they have on hand to do the work, how the skill sets required match with the available resources, and what kind of training or outsourcing may need to be done to round out an incomplete pool of skills. They will also look at the number of hours given resources can devote to the project and the areas of the project resources are best suited to helping with.

5. Estimate durations—Now that the project manager knows what needs to be done, roughly who will be doing it, and in what order, they can go through and estimate the amount of time each task will take to complete, given the resources specified.

6. Develop a schedule—The project schedule can be developed by putting together all of the parts listed, along with the specific schedules of team members, availability of space and equipment, and any hard deadlines that must be met.

Project schedules can be tricky to put together and even harder to maintain. Each project is a unique creation dependent on the many different factors that go into creating the project environment. In working with libraries on their projects, there are a few strategies from across the discipline of project management that are tried and true aids in making project schedules work.

One strategy for successful schedule building is *forward scheduling*. Taken from the critical path method of project management, forward scheduling uses the start date of the project (usually right away) and plots the tasks from there, creating a timeline based on estimated task durations. Once all of the tasks are plotted on a timeline, the project manager can adjust the resources assigned to the tasks to meet external deadlines, account for possible project risks, show a need to add resources, and make realistic promises regarding the project outcomes.

Those who may not be as practiced in project management techniques often begin their schedule at the end. They set a deadline for completion and then "walk back" the schedule from that point. "I'll do task B two weeks before the deadline, and task A one week before that . . ." These are words often heard from inexperienced project managers as they attempt to create a timeline or schedule for their project.

However, backward scheduling is not always a reliable way to make sure that all tasks are accounted for sufficiently to ensure they will be completed on time and up to the quality standards of the project. Backward scheduling leaves very little room for schedule correction when the project schedule begins to slip, as tasks are not begun until the last possible minute. Adding resources to speed up a part of the process must be done on the fly, which can throw off the project budget considerably.

There may be times when backward scheduling makes more sense, especially if it is a very short project with few resources involved. But for major projects involving many stakeholders, it is better to begin with a starting point in the near future and insert tasks into a timeline from that point forward. If there is a predetermined deadline, you can look at the result of this forward scheduling and make adjustments so that the project estimates meet the deadline requirements. If the estimated schedule developed this way runs over the allotted time frame, look for places where resources can be added to speed up a critical task, or make suggestions for adjusting the requirements to meet the time constraint. If the project looks like it will be completed well before the deadline, it can be an opportunity to cut the overall cost of the project by reassigning resources. By telling you when a project can be completed rather than focusing on finishing the project within a predetermined time frame, forward scheduling can help you design more realistic project timelines and customize projects to better fit the needs of the organizations you work with.

Developing Agile project schedules may follow many of the same basic steps as planning a waterfall or critical path project, but the focus with these is on setting up an iterative process that can be improved upon with each repetition. The mantra of agile project management is "fail early, correct course, learn, and improve" (Palmquist et al., 2013). The project schedule is therefore broken into smaller chunks of activity, each of which produces a product and is designed to gather feedback for implementing changes to the process for the next round of tasks. Setting up a schedule for an Agile project is more focused on facilitating a process where the team focuses on improving the process as they go along, not just the product.

Many projects that are not entirely managed using agile principles can benefit from borrowing elements from Agile when creating and maintaining project plans. For example, it is a good idea to incorporate a mechanism for incorporating feedback received during project execution in order to improve processes. Although more traditional project management models emphasize preplanning each task before execution, some room should be left for a small amount of flexibility in response to feedback received while the project is underway.

Two tools that can make project scheduling easier are the *work break-down structure (WBS)* and the *Gantt chart*. The WBS gives the project manager a tool for putting their task list into a logical sequence for execution, define relationships between tasks, and visualizing the way the project must be organized in order to come together. Adding estimated durations to each task in the WBS allows a project manager to chart the real time each task will require for completion, account for dependencies between activities, and get ready to assign resources to complete the tasks.

A WBS is often developed together with a Gantt chart. Gantt charts allow project managers to lay out the work that needs to be done in a visual format that illustrates the duration of each task, shows the major milestones and deadlines of the project, and allows the determination of the project's most essential tasks. They can be an excellent tool for turning all of the information amassed thus far into a project and organize it into a project schedule. When projects are especially complicated, involve the performance of multiple simultaneous tasks, have activities that depend on the completion of previous activities, or demand the time of multiple people who may have other projects or duties at the same time, a Gantt chart can be a lifesaver.

Figure 8.2 shows an example of a partial Gantt chart.

Whereas some projects can be planned and scheduled with a pile of Post-its or an Excel workbook, more complicated projects involving many tasks and resources can be managed much more easily by using technology. A number of project management software applications are available to make scheduling your project and sticking to that schedule easier. Available tools designed to address various project management challenges are continually being developed with many different levels of complexity and at many price points.

Library professionals are often interested in finding software that will help organize and schedule project work, manage the assignment of tasks, and facilitate project communication at the lowest possible cost. Rest assured that many products are out there to meet the needs of libraries, consultants, and individuals alike (Reimers, 2014). You may find that the unique requirements of the projects you work on, as well as the specific needs of the teams involved, necessitate a familiarity with a range of software applications so you can choose the right solutions for each project.

WBS	Task Name	Work	Start	Finish	Predecessor	Resource Name
1	Begin	0 hrs Wed 6/1/16	Wed 6/1/16			
2	Plan Menu	1 hr Wed 6/1/16	Wed 6/1/16	1		
2.1	Plan Menu	1 hr Wed 6/1/16	Wed 6/1/16		Emily[13%]	
3	Grocery Shopping	2.98 hrs Thu 6/2/16	Thu 6/2/16	2		
3.1	Write Shopping list	1 hr Thu 6/2/16	Thu 6/2/16		Emily[13%]	
3.2	Buy Food	1.23 hrs Fri 6/3/16		5		
3.3	Buy Drinks	0.75 hrs Tue 6/7/16		5		
3.3.1	Buy Wine	0.25 hrs Tue 6/7/16	Tue 6/7/16	8	Emily[3%]	
3.3.2	Buy Soda	0.25 hrs Wed 6/8/16	Wed 6/8/16	9	Chris[3%]	
3.3.3	Buy Coffee	0.25 hrs Thu 6/9/16	Thu 6/9/16	12	Chris[3%]	
4	Prepare Meal	3.25 hrs Fri 6/10/16	Fri 6/10/16	4		
4.1	Prepare Entree	2.25 hrs Fri 6/10/16				
4.1.1	Chop Vegetables	0.25 hrs Fri 6/10/16	Fri 6/10/16	4	Chris[3%]	
4.1.2	Cook Chicken	2 hrs Mon 6/13/16	Mon 6/13/16	16	Emily[25%]	
4.2	Prepare Salad	0.75 hrs Mon 6/13/16				
4.2.1	Wash Vegetables	0.25 hrs Mon 6/13/16	Mon 6/13/16	16	Robert[3%]	
4.2.2	Cut Vegetables	0.25 hrs Tue 6/14/16	Tue 6/14/16	19	Chris[3%]	
4.2.3	Toss Salad	0.25 hrs Wed 6/15/16	Wed 6/15/16	20	Chris[3%]	
4.3	Slice Bread	0.25 hrs Tue 6/14/16	Tue 6/14/16	17	Emily[3%]	
5	Set table	0.75 hrs Tue 6/14/16	Tue 6/14/16			
5.1	Lay tablecloth	0.25 hrs Tue 6/14/16	Tue 6/14/16	19	Emily[3%]	
5.2	Place Settings	0.5 hrs Wed 6/15/16				

FIGURE 8.2. Sample Gantt Chart

Challenges in Scheduling

One additional project management challenge faced by most consultants is the management of several simultaneous or overlapping projects. Managing multiple projects involving different clients can be a daunting proposition and requires a high degree of skill in scheduling and time management. When scheduling consulting project activities, it is essential to keep an eye on the schedules of the other projects you have undertaken, delegating or delaying tasks whenever necessary to keep all of your projects on track.

The picture becomes even more complex when you are leading a project team as part of your consulting job. Teams of resources within your consulting group may need to be shared between different projects and their time allocated accordingly. Working together with other consultants can help reduce workload and extend your reach within the library market, but it makes coordination of projects critical. Strong internal communication and a collaborative project management process can help you avoid issues arising from scheduling conflicts and resource overallocation.

Teams within the organization that hired you will also have other duties that they need to perform as part of their regular jobs and may be overallocated with the combination of normal responsibilities and added project work. This is a situation you may face frequently as library staff, who are already spread thin, are placed in a position where project work is seen as secondary to the work assigned by their regular supervisors. Without any control over the other activities your project resources are tasked with, it can be difficult to make sure that your schedule is designed in a way that makes completion of work possible given the resources you have to work with.

Coordinating project work for yourself, your team, and all stakeholders is essential for any consultant who wants to remain both solvent and sane. Planning overlapping projects in coordination with one another to minimize Gantt charts for your various projects can be very useful in helping to determine times when your attention needs to be focused on the activities of a project with a particular client. Comparing Gantt charts for your projects will help you create a schedule where spikes in your anticipated workload do not coincide.

Communication

Possibly the most important skills consultants and project managers can cultivate to ensure success are communication skills. Clear, consistent, appropriate communication can make or break a project and keep a consultant in business. Without exceptional communication, it is impossible to establish stakeholder expectations, set project goals, get work done efficiently, or come to agreements on the final status or quality of project deliverables.

Communication is also much more complex than we tend to think. Many professionals who consider themselves good communicators make the mistake of underestimating the challenge of maintaining communication during the planning and execution of a project. As part of their formal training, all Project Management Professionals must learn the following formula for calculating the number of communication channels in a given project:

$$n(n-1)/2$$

In this equation, "n" represents the number of stakeholders involved in a project. A project involving only two people is simple: there is only one communication channel. Add a few more people to the mix, however, and the picture changes dramatically.

Say you have been hired as a consultant to help redesign a library Web site. A number of different stakeholders are involved in this job in addition to you. There's the library director, the heads of the various departments, and the two Web developers who work with you. This brings us to a total of seven people. Applying the formula presented earlier, you'll see there are already 21 possible communication channels to establish and maintain.

But the immediate project team is not made up of only the stakeholders. Information about this project must be both disseminated to and received from the rest of the library staff (20 more people), the library trustees (7 more people), and the leaders of the library's Friends group (5 more people). So far, that's 39 people, for a total of 741 communication channels.

$$39(39-1)/2 = 741$$

And you haven't even counted the stakeholder groups within the community yet! What happens when you consider that the changes you make to the Web site need to be communicated to the local teachers, lawmakers, community groups, and the general patron population? The number of communication channels to be considered can easily balloon into the thousands with a public-facing project.

Not only are there a surprising number of communication channels to maintain in most projects, there are also many considerations that go into deciding how to best maintain those channels. When planning a project, it is important to consider the methods used for communicating with each stakeholder group, the kinds of information that will be included in communication via these various modes, the frequency of communications, and the level of detail that will be communicated. These factors may change throughout the project lifecycle and may need to be addressed in terms of the information that must be communicated during the various project phases.

Managing this requires the development of a *communication plan*. You should never embark upon a project without having at least some form of communication plan in place to help guide your project team and other stakeholders through the process. A strong communication plan will establish everyone's expectations for what will be communicated, when, by whom, by what means, and at what level of detail. Establishing this at the beginning of a project can mean the difference between a smooth, successful project and one that falters almost immediately.

Most communication plans are based directly on the stakeholder register and RACI matrix. By the time these documents are in place, you will have a pretty good idea of the project goals and objectives and can look at the whole package to determine the project's communication needs. These needs can then be written into a plan that outlines every major aspect of how communication will be handled throughout the duration of the project.

With more complex projects, it is sometimes helpful to create a communication matrix to help define and illustrate the relationships between stakeholders and the ways they can expect to give and receive information. This is very similar to a RACI matrix, with each stakeholder group being matched with communication methods, frequency, depth of detail, and who is responsible for this communication.

Table 8.1 shows an example of a very simple partial communication matrix.

The communication matrix can then be summarized into a written communication plan to be reviewed and approved by the project sponsor, either as part of a larger project plan or as a separate planning document. For most projects, the communication plan is one of the most vital documents of the entire project. Focus your early project communications on disseminating the communication plan and eliciting feedback on it. Communicating on

TABLE 8.1. Sample Communication Matrix

	Information	Method	Frequency	Detail	Responsibility
Director	Project Status Update	E-mail	Weekly	Overview	Project Manager
Board Members	Project Status Update	E-mail	Weekly	Overview	Project Manager
Project Team	Project Status Update	Meeting	Weekly	Detail by Responsibility Area	Project Manager
Circulation Staff	Project Status Update	E-mail	Every Other Week	Progress Summary	Team Lead
Reference Staff	Project Status Update	E-mail	Every Other Week	Progress Summary	Team Lead
Community Groups	Policy Change Notice	E-mail	Two Times	Explanation of New Policy and Procedures	Project Manager/ Director
Other Staff	Project Status Update	E-mail	Every Other Week	Progress Summary	Team Lead
General Community	Announce- ment	Newsletter	One Time	Write Up of New Service	Project Manager/ Director

communication may seem like overkill, but the importance of establishing an understanding about the way information will be shared cannot be underestimated.

BUILDING YOUR TOOLBOX

Even if you do not completely adopt a formal project management framework for your consulting work, there are many ways in which incorporating just a few practices and tools can help you improve your productivity and project success rate. Library consulting can often feel like an exercise in cat herding, and it can be difficult to get the job done when the pressure is on. Looking at the ways professional project managers initiate their projects, set the scope, develop schedules, and plan for effective communication can offer a consultant a good starting point for getting a handle on the workload they undertake.

Tools and techniques developed by successful project managers are often easily transferred into the world of consulting and may offer solutions to some of the most daunting problems we consultants face. It is important to keep an open mind when examining these techniques and be creative about the ways we might adapt these techniques to the unique situations we find ourselves dealing with. Over time, project management strategies can be reimagined and recombined to provide you with a customized set of tools that work for you and the types of consulting jobs you specialize in.

RESOURCES

Berkun, Scott. *Making Things Happen: Mastering Project Management*. Revised edition. O'Reilly Media, 2008.

Carew, Michael. *RACI Matrix How To*. https://www.youtube.com/watch?v=qsPu1b8lcRQ

Carlson, Eric. *Project Management: From Conception to Practice*. CreateSpace Independent Publishing Platform, 2016.

Craig, Juana Clark. *Project Management Lite: Just Enough to Get the Job Done . . . Nothing More*. 10/22/12 edition. CreateSpace Independent Publishing Platform, 2012.

Fremouw, Belinda. "Enterprise Environmental Factors versus Organizational Process Assets (CONCEPT 12) | Passionate Project Management." Blog. *Passionate Project Management*. May 15, 2011. https://www.passionatepm.com/blog/enterprise-environmental-factors-versus-organizational-process-assets-pmp-concept-12

Heagney, Joseph, and James P. Lewis. *Fundamentals of Project Management*. 4th edition. AMACOM, 2012.

Heerkens, Gary. *Project Management*. 2nd edition. McGraw-Hill Education, 2014. Briefcase Books Series.

Kelly, Eric Damian. "Choosing a Consultant Part 5. Managing the Project." *American Planning Association*. https://www.planning.org/consultants/choosing/part5.htm

Kogon, Kory. *Project Management for the Unofficial Project Manager*. BenBella Books, 2015.

Lebedeva, Anna. "Five Essential Project Management Skills for RM and IG Professionals." *Information Management Journal* 49.5 (2015): 28–33.

Palmquist, Steve, Mary Ann Lapham, Suzanne Garcia-Miller, Timothy A. Chick, and Ipek Ozkaya. "Parallel Worlds: Agile and Waterfall Differences and Similarities." *Research Showcase @ CMU*. Carnegie Mellon University Software Institute, 2013. https://resources.sei.cmu.edu/asset_files/TechnicalNote/2013_004_001_62918.pdf

PMI | Project Management Institute. https://www.pmi.org

Project Management Institute. *A Guide to the Project Management Body of Knowledge (PMBOK® Guide)–Fifth Edition.* Project Management Institute, 2013.

Project Scheduling Best Practices in an Agile Environment. http://innovategov.org/2016/02/05/project-scheduling-best-practices-in-an-agile-environment/

ProjectManagement.com—Templates. https://www.projectmanagement.com/templates/

Reimers, Frances. "50 Project Management Tools for Freelance Consultants." *Zintro Blog.* November 20, 2014. https://blog.zintro.com/2014/11/20/50-project-management-tools-freelance-consultants/

Roberts, Paul. *Guide to Project Management: Getting It Right and Achieving Lasting Benefit.* 2nd edition. John Wiley & Sons Inc., 2013.

Samanen, James. "Project Management for Consultants | Project Leader Solutions." *Project Leader Solutions.* http://www.projectleadersolutions.com/project-management-for-consultants/

Sutherland, Jeff. *Scrum: The Art of Doing Twice the Work in Half the Time.* Crown Business, 2014.

Turner, Arthur N. "Consulting Is More Than Giving Advice." *Harvard Business Review.* https://hbr.org/1982/09/consulting-is-more-than-giving-advice

White, Karen R. J., and Pamela Puleo. *Practical Project Management for Agile Nonprofits: Approaches and Templates to Help You Manage with Limited Resources.* Maven House, 2013.

Epilogue

A Few Last Things Before You Begin Your Journey

Melissa M. Powell, BiblioEase

We started out this book with the questions: *"So you want to be a consultant? Now what?"* Hopefully by the time you have gotten to this point you have the answer to the first and, if you answered *yes*, a good start on the second. As you start to build your business, you will come up against unique situations, especially if you have chosen to do something new and different. The goal of this book is to give you the tools to choose the right path for you, get started more easily, and find solutions to any of the situations that may arise. However, there are a few more things that could help you.

FIND A MENTOR

One of the most useful things you can do at this point is to find a mentor (or two). Find someone who is doing what you want to do or who you admire and ask if they would be willing to answer questions for you or to be available to bounce ideas off of. A mentor is one of the handiest tools in your toolbox because they are there for you! This may be a short-term exchange or a lifetime partnership. You may have more than one mentor, depending on what you are focusing on at the moment: someone to work with on the ins and outs of consulting and someone who focuses on something more specific that you find yourself working on. In the consulting business, mentoring can also have the benefit of partnership on projects or contracts and lead to a wonderful business relationship.

As in any relationship there are things to look for in a good mentor. They should be able to not only give advice, but give impartial advice. A good mentor will have your best interests at heart, not theirs. They are not trying to make you another version of themselves but a strong and independent consultant of your own. They are there to support you, assist with professional development, give you tips for solving problems, and encourage you to make decisions and reflect on your own work.

As you work through your new career, you may find that your mentor changes. You meet new people, change your focus, or outgrow your mentor. These are natural and encouraged. You may also find that the person you thought would be a great mentor is not. Don't be afraid to move on. You also don't need to be best friends with your mentor or even work with them on jobs.

As you grow more successful and gain a reputation in your particular consulting field, you will find yourself in the position to mentor other consultants. Do it. It is as beneficial to mentor as it is to be mentored. Especially in this field, where a large part of the job is to mentor and coach librarians through projects, strategic planning, change management, etc., consultants are naturals at mentoring. As you can see from this book, consultants help each other because it not only makes the library consulting business better, but it makes the consultants better too.

CERTIFICATIONS

A common question asked by new consultants or those considering consulting is whether they need certifications. You do not need to have certifications to be a library consultant, especially if you have proven skills in the industry. However, you may decide to pursue a certification to enhance your toolbox and/or expand your reach. Many for-profit agencies offer certifications, as do nonprofit educational institutions, such as community colleges.

In most professions there are associations that are recognized within the industries they serve and they will focus on particular certifications. Just like the American Library Association (ALA) accredits Library and Information Studies (LIS) programs, these associations may even offer their own certifications. You will want to ensure that the certification you earn is one that is recognized and valued with the client base you are serving. In the library world, hiring agents look for the ALA-accredited MLIS, and you wouldn't waste time and money attending a nonaccredited program—the same goes for other certifications or programs. These take time and money, so don't waste your time and money on one that will mean nothing to your customers.

A FEW MORE TOOLS FOR YOUR TOOLBOX

Many basic skills will come to the forefront as you begin working in your new chosen profession. You assessed your skills in Bolt and Bishoff's

Chapter 1 and hopefully learned some new skills in the chapters following. As you begin working as a consultant, you will find that you are always learning and honing your craft. It's part of the fun of being a consultant!

Here are some basic skills often considered to be core for the independent library consultant.

Project Management

You learned about project management in Emily Clasper's Chapter 8, "Getting It Done: Project Management Tips for Library Consultants." This chapter just touched on the tip of the iceberg of what project management is—enough to get you started in using and understanding it. Some consultants concentrate on being project managers specifically and are able to work on any kind of project. If this is something you think you want to do, you might consider getting your PMI Certification.

Certification in Project Management

If you decide to pursue a certification in project management, there are several types; the most recognized in all industries is the Project Management Professional (PMP) offered by the Project Management Institute. To qualify as a PMP you must meet the following prerequisites as well as pass the exam:

- Secondary degree (high school diploma, associate's degree or the global equivalent)
- 7,500 hours leading and directing projects
- 35 hours of project management education

OR

- Four-year degree
- 4,500 hours leading and directing projects
- 35 hours of project management education

The exam is based on the Project Management Body of Knowledge (PMBOK) and consists of 200 multiple-choice questions that must be answered in four hours. To maintain the PMP you must earn 60 professional development units (PDUs) every three years. It is a hearty investment of time and money; however, if you really want to broaden your skills and reach, you may find it worth your while.

FACILITATION AND PROBLEM SOLVING

Facilitation and problem solving are the backbone of consulting, especially if you are concentrating on the areas of strategic planning, workflow, etc. Even training and presenting encompass each of these, as you will need to be able to think on the spot and encourage others to think as well.

Look through the literature and you will find everything from 3 to 10 basic principles of effective facilitating. It can be overwhelming! Basically, a facilitator is a guide or coach, not a sage. You don't give opinions; you draw out the opinions and ideas of the group members. The focus of facilitation is how people learn or progress in their planning, not the final result. The role of facilitator is as a neutral party. You never take sides.

A good consultant leads from behind. You are encouraging the organization to solve the problem, adding in a few suggestions and tools for them to use, but you want them to learn from the process so they can continue with the progress on their own. The best solution is the one that works for their organization, and for that it, needs to come from the organization. You can offer suggestions; however, in the end, it must be their decision, their choice.

What does a facilitator do? They make sure everyone has an opportunity to participate by creating a structure that allows for everyone's ideas to be heard and supported. They discourage criticism of ideas and make sure that the group feels that the ideas and decisions are theirs.

The best facilitators encourage sessions of no-holds-barred brainstorming to begin the process; the more fantastic, the better. This helps free up the group from self-constraints and allows for a better flow of ideas. Often participants think their solution or idea is really *out there* when in reality it is right in line with the organization and a sustainable practice! A few little tweaks, and you are off and running. Anything that gets people to stop being afraid of sharing their ideas for fear of criticism or ridicule is in order.

Facilitation versus Training

Often a consultant will find themselves in a situation where they must facilitate or even train to move forward in a project. Facilitation and training do overlap; however, they are not the same thing.

The *International Association of Facilitators (IAF)* explains it this way:

The trainer comes in with both the process and the content. They have content expertise and specific content to cover, and they decide how the content will be covered: the process.

The facilitator controls the process yet does not provide content. They work with the client to define the session purpose and output, such as a strategic plan. A facilitator can even function with no content knowledge. Their role is helping the group manage the knowledge they have or can access to achieve the result (*IAF*, https://www.iaf-world.org/site/professional/cpf).

If a serious conflict arises, you may need a mediator. A mediator is a neutral party whose process is to assist in negotiations that lead to a binding and enforceable agreement to settle a dispute. They are also referred to as an arbitrator. Because this usually involves a conflict strong enough to call in a third party and leads to a generally legal result, training and certification is highly recommended.

As a facilitator you must be aware of various communication skills, such as open body language, appropriate eye contact, deep listening, body language (yours and others), avoiding confrontation, asking open questions, and above all, being genuine. These skills also do you well in all aspects of consulting.

Taking workshops in emotional intelligence or other soft skills can help you in this area, along with the advice on networking mentioned in Schimpf's Chapter 6.

Certification in Facilitation Skills

A certification is not necessary to act as a facilitator; however, if you do desire one, many different agencies offer certification. The International Association of Facilitators (IAF) offers the IAF Certified Professional Facilitator designation (IAF, https://www.iaf-world.org/site/professional/Becoming %20a%20CPF). As with many professional certifications, assessment of current knowledge and experience is a part of the process.

PRESENTING, TEACHING, AND TRAINING SKILLS

Many independent information professionals get their start in presenting or training. You have a unique expertise, and people want to learn from you. As mentioned in previous chapters, you might start out by doing presentations or workshops at your local library conferences to get experience. This can lead to paid opportunities at libraries, preconferences, or other organizations.

The library world is changing at a rapid pace. There is a growing demand for skilled people to train, present, and educate staff in the new technologies, cataloging and metadata standards, and programming, as well as the good old standbys of customer service, collection management, and management. Everything from one-time workshops to asynchronous weeks-long courses is in demand. Knowing how to pass along knowledge—correctly—to a variety of learners is a valuable skill.

Even if you have no plans to teach or train, you may find yourself being asked to present workshops, give keynotes, or conduct other speaking engagements as your reputation grows as a subject matter expert. Understanding how to convey information to groups of people is always valuable.

Adult Learners

To be a successful presenter or trainer, you need to be engaging and effective. Teaching adults is different from teaching children. As discussed in Wagner's Chapter 3, there are several reasons why adults seek out learning. Many just love to learn for learning's sake, whereas others are seeking out education to fill in gaps from library school or to upgrade their skills. Then there are the individuals and groups that are doing it not by choice, but as a mandate from their employer. You need to be able to create programs that will work for all of these groups and learning styles, whether online or in person.

Eduard Lindeman, one of the pioneers in the field of adult education, defined five main characteristics of adult learning:

- Adults are motivated to learn as they experience needs and interests that learning will satisfy.
- Adults' orientation to learning is life centered.
- Experience is the richest source for adults' learning.
- Adults have a deep need to be self-directing.
- Individual differences among people increase with age. (Knowles, Holton, & Swanson, 2005)

Adult learning is goal oriented or driven by a need. Whether it is to learn new skills, brush up on current ones, or to move into something entirely different in their career, the learner has a goal. You need to be aware of those goals at the beginning and ensure that you meet all or most of them. This can be done through preworkshop surveys, informal polls, or just having them state their goals as part of an introduction.

The presenter/trainer needs to respect the knowledge and life experiences of the workshop or class participants as part of the learning process. Encourage learners to connect past experiences with what they are learning. You need to be able to draw out their experiences, whether they think it is relevant or not, and apply them to what they are currently learning. Above all, respect that they already know things, especially for the participants who are there as a mandate. They will come in feeling that you have nothing of value to add to their knowledge or that they have an experience unlike anything you are familiar with.

Adult learners are self-directed or autonomous. They are actively involved in the learning process, and they make choices relevant to their learning objectives. They need to be responsible for their workload and to be proactive in setting their goals. Each may be in your workshop for a different reason, but in the end they each get what they need.

Learning should be relevant, both to the learner's goals and to the topic at hand. Real-world examples and tips that can be immediately applied to their situations are vital to engaging and effective learning. Participants who see that what you are saying is more than theory and actually works in the real world are more likely to participate and actually leave with new ideas and practices.

In that same vein, keeping things practical and approachable leads to more success in learning. It is okay to teach theory as long as it is completely related to something practical. The theory should explain the *why* of the *what*. This cannot be emphasized enough. Teach what you know because you have done it and you know it works!

Finally, avoid just being the "sage on the stage." Encourage collaboration among the participants and with yourself. These are your colleagues, and you will learn from them as they learn from you.

PRESENTATION TECHNIQUES

Lecture

Combine various styles of teaching in your workshops, seminars, and training. It's okay to do a little lecturing, but limit it to 15 to 20 minutes at a time, with learning activities in between. You want to make sure people not only get what you have said, but are ready for the next bit of information you are going to present them.

Beware of dependence on slides. "Death by PowerPoint" is a common phrase used among trainers and presenters. Look it up on Google, and you will find numerous articles and pages dedicated to avoiding the mind-numbing boredom that is often associated with workshops. Even worse is the fact that these are usually darkened rooms so the slides can be seen. If you end up being the presenter after lunch, you are doomed!

Basically, create a consistent look, make the slide engaging by using it to enhance a point, limit the text on the slide, use storytelling (don't read your slides!), and have a focused message. Watch some TED Talks for great ways to use slides appropriately to enhance the visual aspects of your presentation. Often people use their slide decks as a handout. Microsoft PowerPoint makes this easy by giving you a layout option with room for notes. Don't do it. Create actual handouts with useful information. Your slides should not be able to replace a good and informative handout and will be much more useful to the participants.

Discussion

Encouraging periods of discussion in your workshops and training will help the participants retain the information. Present them with a scenario or a problem and facilitate their problem-solving process; then summarize the process and the solution(s). Depending on the topic you are presenting, have the participants come with questions or projects in hand and spend time working out the problem. This works well with a technical topic such as cataloging.

Use questions as learning tools. Break up the participants into pairs or smaller groups and present a question that requires critical thinking. Allow them to discuss for a few minutes and bring the group back together. Have them share what they discovered. Make connections between points, ask more questions, and summarize key points. Come back to the question and apply what they discovered through their discussion.

Demonstration

An effective way to teach is to demonstrate what is being taught. This is particularly important if you are conducting specific training, such as cataloging, database usage, or even customer service. If possible include hands-on experience for the participants. Many people learn better by doing.

Online Learning or E-Learning

In this day and age, a lot of training and learning are done in the virtual environment. Many libraries and organizations find that it is more cost and time effective to have classes and one-off workshops presented online for their staff, either live or recorded. Many consultants specialize in virtual learning. The basic learning and presenting skills apply, with the added layer of making up for the loss of nonverbal cues. You cannot rely on the yawn, the eye roll, the fidgeting, or the nodding to cue you in to which direction you need to take the workshop.

You need to be more skilled at encouraging conversation, whether in a chat box, on a phone line, in texts, or however the platform encourages it. Use interactive boards or other collaborative software. Stop for questions every 15 to 20 minutes to check in with everyone. Use whatever interactive tools the platform has, such as polls or quizzes. Make the presentation engaging and entertaining. You should be doing this anyway, however, because you are limited in your ability to interact on a more personal level; you need to be even more engaging to hold their attention.

You might work with an existing organization that provides course management software and instructional design in a formal asynchronized course format, or you might be doing slide presentations for a group using something like GoToMeeting or WebEx.

Included in the resources are some helpful books on the subject of teaching online. Various associations also offer regular courses and workshops on the skills needed, especially those dedicated to training and education.

CERTIFICATION IN WORKSHOP AND TRAINING SKILLS

The Association for Talent Development (ATD) is a professional membership organization that offers a Certified Professional in Learning and Performance (CPLP) credential for training and development practitioners. It is a broad-based certification and addresses 10 areas of expertise as defined by the ATD Competency Model. ATD supports those who develop the knowledge and skills of employees in organizations around the world. The association was previously known as the American Society for Training & Development (ASTD). They offer many different learning and certification programs that are in line with the work of library consultants. If you are interested in learning more and/or getting some certifications under your belt, they probably have what you are looking for.

WHAT IS YOUR PASSION?

As you prepare yourself for your new career as an independent information professional, never forget the reason you chose this particular career in the first place: your passion for libraries and information. Check back in with yourself as you form your company, start off on projects, and network. Tap into that excitement to keep you going through the tedious parts of being a small business owner. Remember to be that consultant with a commitment to being helpful, honest, curious, and with the right caring attitude, and you will be a successful and satisfied independent information professional!

RESOURCES

Andler, Nicolai. *Tools for Project Management, Workshops and Consulting*. 3rd edition. Publicis, 2016.

Association for Talent Development. https://www.td.org/

Brounstein, Marty. *Coaching & Mentoring for Dummies*. Wiley, 2000.

Carroll, Michael. *The Mindful Leader: Ten Principles for Bringing out the Best in Ourselves and Others*. Trumpeter, 2007.

International Association of Facilitators (IAF). https://www.iaf-world.org/site/

Knowles, Malcom, Elwood Holton, and Richard Swanson. *The Adult Learner: The Definitive Classic in Adult Education and Human Resource Development*. Elsevier, 2005.

Merriam, Sharan. B. *Learning in Adulthood: A Comprehensive Guide*. 3rd edition. Jossey-Bass, 2007.

Nokes, Sebastian. *The Definitive Guide to Project Management*. 2nd edition. Financial Times/Prentice Hall, 2007.

Project Management Institute. *A Guide to the Project Management Body of Knowledge (PMBOK® Guide)*. 5th edition. Project Management Institute, 2013.

Project Management Institute. http://www.pmi.org/

Project Management Institute Seminars World. *Project Management: Competencies and Structure Including an Introduction to PMI's Guide to the Project Management Body of Knowledge (PMBOK® Guide)*. Project Management Institute Seminars World, 2014.

Ragan, Lawrence. *Best Practice in Online Teaching*. CreateSpace Independent Publishing Platform, 2015.

Schein, Edgar H. *Helping: How to Offer, Give, and Receive Help*. Berrett-Koehler, 2009.

Schein, Edgar H. *Humble Consulting: How to Provide Real Help Faster*. Berrett-Koehler, 2016.

Smith, Robin. M. *Conquering the Content: A Blueprint for Online Course Design and Development*. Jossey-Bass, 2014.

Appendix A

Specific Types of Consulting
(as listed on libraryconsultants.org)

Accessibility
Adult Services
Archives and Preservation
Automation
Board Development
Children and Teen Facilities
Coaching
Communication Development
Community Analysis & GIS
Compensation & Performance
 Management
Continuous Improvement
Database Design
Design Services
Digitization
Disaster Planning
Evaluation
Executive Search
Facilitation
Facilities Planning
Focus Groups
Fundraising & Development
Grant Writing

HR Audit/Study
Innovation
Joint Use Libraries
Leadership Development
Management
Marketing Plans
Needs Assessment
Organizational Design
Planning for Results
Policy Development
Program Planning
Recruitment and Retention
Speaking
Staff Development & Training
Strategic Planning
Surveys
Team Building
Technology Management
Technology Planning
Technology Training
Teen Services
Website Design and Usability
Workflow Analysis

Appendix B
ASCLA Library Consultants Code of Ethics

The Association of Specialized & Cooperative Library Agencies (ASCLA—a division of the American Library Association [ALA]) has adopted a voluntary code of ethics for consultants. Inspired by a similar code from the Institute for Management Consultants, Nancy Bolt adapted the list to fit the needs of libraries.

The purpose of this code is to help library consultants maintain their professionalism and adhere to high ethical standards as they provide services to clients and in their dealings with their colleagues and in their commitment to the public and the library profession. The individual members must use their judgment to apply these principles. Consultants voluntarily agree to abide by this code of ethics. ASCLA does not enforce the code. This code is offered as a supplement to the ALA code of ethics and is not intended to supplant it.

1. I will serve my clients with integrity, competence, independence, objectivity, and professionalism.

2. I will only accept assignments for which I possess the requisite experience and competence to perform and will only assign staff or engage colleagues with the knowledge and expertise needed to serve my clients effectively.

3. Before accepting any engagement, I will ensure that I have worked with my clients to establish a mutual understanding of the benefits, results, objectives, scope, work plan, and timetable.

4. I will agree in advance with a client on the basis for fees and expenses and will charge fees that are reasonable and commensurate with the services delivered and the responsibility accepted.

5. I will treat appropriately all confidential client information that is not public knowledge, take reasonable steps to prevent it from access by

unauthorized people, and will not take advantage of proprietary or privileged information, either for use by myself, the client's organization, or another client, without the client's permission.

6. I will respect the rights of consulting colleagues and consulting firms and will not use their proprietary information or methodologies without permission.

7. I will avoid conflicts of interest or the appearance of such and will immediately disclose to the client circumstances or interests that I believe may influence my judgment or objectivity.

8. I will offer to withdraw from a consulting assignment when I believe my objectivity or integrity may be impaired.

9. I will not accept commissions, remuneration, or other benefits from a third party in connection with recommendations to a client without that client's prior knowledge and consent, and I will disclose in advance any financial interests in goods or services that form part of such recommendations.

10. If within the scope of my engagement, I will report to appropriate authorities within or external to the client organization any occurrences deemed to be of malfeasance, dangerous behavior, or illegal activities.

11. I will advertise my services without deception and without misrepresentation or denigration of individual consulting practitioners, consulting firms, or the consulting profession.

12. I will represent the library profession with integrity and professionalism in my relations with my clients, colleagues, and the general public.

This Code of Ethics is based on a code developed by the Institute of Management Consultants (IMC). We thank IMC for their permission to use their code as the basis of this code.

Reprinted with permission from the Association of Specialized & Cooperative Agencies.

About the Editor and Contributors

EDITOR

MELISSA M. POWELL has been working as a library consultant and contractor for over 10 years, having spent the previous 27 working in public, academic, and special libraries. As the owner of BiblioEase, she has worked with libraries and consortia teaching cataloging, customer service, and collection management. Being an independent professional has allowed her many varied opportunities from working as webcast producer for Publishers Weekly to editing an international technical newsletter.

Melissa has been active as a mentor for librarians and library students for many years and finds sharing knowledge one of the most rewarding experiences there is.

CONTRIBUTORS

LIZ BISHOFF, of The Bishoff Group, is an experienced consultant who provides management consulting services to libraries, museums, and other cultural heritage organizations and cooperatives that support these organizations. Her consulting services focus on digital library initiatives, creating and managing sustainable organizations, digital preservation, business planning, and grant development.

Together Liz and Nancy Bolt lead *Assembling Your Consultants Toolkit,* a popular workshop on becoming a library consultant.

CARSON BLOCK, of Carson Block Consulting, has led, managed, and supported library technology efforts for more than 20 years. Carson brings a user-centered technological perspective, with an emphasis on solutions that are both transparent and powerful, with some "gee whiz" thrown into the mix. Carson is the instructor for the ALA-APA Management of Technology course.

Carson's passions include leading technology visioning and planning, creating highly functional work groups, technical design (including infrastructure, RFID, points of self-service, and more), and project management with a focus on technology solutions that powerfully serve the impacts each library has in the community it serves.

NANCY BOLT, of Nancy Bolt & Associates, is a respected consultant and mentor. Bolt, a retired Colorado State librarian, is the co-creator of the ALA-APA Library Support Staff Certification Program, which provides a practical curriculum that has allowed numerous library support staff to advance in the workplace, and created the *ASCLA Library Consultant Code of Ethics*. Nancy made significant contributions to the success of the E-Rate program when she chaired the first ALA E-Rate Task Force. Additionally, work that she carried out ultimately contributed to the Bill & Melinda Gates Foundation funding the Broadband Technology Opportunities Projects, which had a profound effect on libraries across the country. In 2016, she received the ALA Elizabeth Futas Catalyst for Change Award.

EMILY CLASPER is a librarian, project manager, speaker, trainer, and consultant living on Long Island in New York. She has worked for the Suffolk Cooperative Library System since 2005, helping to provide cooperative services and technical support to 54 public libraries. She is a certified Project Management Professional (PMP), often coordinating large cooperative projects for the libraries in her consortium and offering her project planning and development skills to libraries seeking assistance in making great ideas come to life.

A Library Journal Mover and Shaker (2012), Emily is a charismatic and engaging speaker, having presented at many local events, as well as library conferences at both the state and national level. A creative leader and change agent dedicated to helping library staff at all levels gain confidence with new skills, her training workshops are known for being fun and making tough topics approachable. Above all, Emily is an all-around troublemaker who spends her free time keeping her equally mischievous children (Robert, 11 and Claire, 8) from burning the house down.

JAMIE HOLLIER, along with Tynan Szvetecz and Jen Chang, manages Commerce Kitchen and Anneal, Inc. They are passionate about the future of work. Traditional business practices place profits over prosperity, middle management over autonomy, and assembly-line thinking over holistic thinking. As co-founders and executives at Commerce Kitchen and Anneal, Inc., they believe in prosperity, employee autonomy, creative thinking, risk taking, and the power of open communication.

At Commerce Kitchen and Anneal, they cook up software. Commerce Kitchen is a dev studio that began in 2003, with a focus on digital health, education, and workflow automation platforms. Anneal started in 2012 with a focus on providing the business analysis, strategic foresight, and technical skills needed to successfully plan and execute digital initiatives for libraries, nongovernmental organizations (NGOs), education, government, and more. They are skilled designers, developers, and strategists who architect high-performance Web sites, offer ongoing production support, Health Insurance Portability and Accountability Act (HIPAA) security compliance, and user engagement strategy.

Jamie was honored as a White House Champion of Change in 2013. Since 2014 Commerce Kitchen has been chosen for the Small Company of the Year Award from the Colorado Women's Chamber for three years running and in 2015 was a winner of Colorado Companies to Watch and Best Places to Work. In 2016, they were a top 10 winner for Colorado's Healthiest Employers.

CRYSTAL SCHIMPF is the principal training consultant for Kixal, a training and instructional design firm. Crystal is a librarian and a trainer, with a passion for instructional design and technology. As founder of Kixal, she provides innovative, transformative training for libraries and nonprofits using proven techniques for the best in online and in-person learning experiences. She has provided training on projects for the Urban Libraries Council's Edge Initiative, the Public Library Association, TechSoup, Infopeople, the Washington State Library, the Colorado State Library, Community Technology Network, and the R-Squared Conference.

DENISE SHOCKLEY, as a teacher, librarian, and CPA, has always been passionate about connecting people. With over 25 years of working with a wide range of ages, across a variety of organizations, the common thread is people, processes, and potential.

From what started as a curiosity about how she could help libraries incorporate cost–benefit analysis into new processes, Denise became captivated with the flow of the accounting cycle. Much like a librarian, accountants identify, evaluate, and connect information in a meaningful way that tells a story. The accounting cycle connects what appear to be independent transactions into a meaningful report that tells the financial story of the business. Energized by this challenge, what started as a plan to take one accounting course led to becoming a CPA.

Denise's approach to accounting has been with the heart of a teacher and the resourcefulness of a librarian. She is in the process of transitioning to consulting as she continues to blend her background and experiences to connect people with information, processes, and potential.

MELISSA STOCKTON is a consultant and founding member at The Quipu Group, a library software, products, services, and ILS consulting firm. She has many years of experience in technical services and ILS migration and regularly consults with libraries and consortia on a variety of projects. As the primary consultant, Melissa regularly assists individual libraries and library consortia in writing their RFPs for ILS migration, dealing with the prospective vendors, providing analysis, and handling every aspect of system procurement and implementation.

TYNAN SZVETECZ is the CEO and a co-founder, with Jamie Hollis, of the innovation studio, Commerce Kitchen, which engineers complex mobile and web applications for the healthcare and nonprofit sectors. In the past 14 years, Commerce Kitchen has grown to an award-winning company recognized in the community for its fair and equal treatment of women, for which it won the 2014 Small Company of the Year Award from the Colorado Women's Chamber, and it has been among the winners of Best Places to Work three years running for 2014, 2015, and 2016. Its award-winning projects have revolutionized how populations become more digitally literate and how healthcare can be revolutionized through telemedicine and interoperability.

Tynan is a lifelong learner who has doggedly pursued interests exploring music, computer science, the art of cooking, blind-tasting wine, and the study of how innovations in technology and social trends influence each other.

Over the last 20 years, he has studied flamenco guitar at Berklee College of Music in Boston, acquired a Personal Chef Certificate in Boulder, Colorado, and become a Candidate for Guild Master Sommelier through the International Wine & Spirits Guild. In his pursuit of understanding how future trends emerge and influence business, society, and culture, he acquired a Certificate in Strategic Forecasting from the University of Houston, a program commonly associated with NASA.

PAT WAGNER has been a trainer, educator, and consultant for 40 years, having worked with clients in 48 states and Canada. She is a manager and producer at Pattern Research, Inc., and an educator and producer at Siera: Learn. Teach. Inspire. Pat likes to find the essence in models of human behavior and organizational design and build effective and engaging formats for learning: face to face, in print, and online. She has been a poet, playwright, printer, publisher, and graphic designer and loves books, gardens, and the arts.

Index